God's Path for Selecting a *Love That Lasts*

Selective Dating without the Heartaches and Dangers

Leah Weber Heling

Milwaukee, Wisconsin

God's Path for Selecting a Love That Lasts
Selective Dating without the Heartaches and Dangers

© 2018 by Leah Weber Heling

All rights reserved. No part of this book may be reproduced, transmitted in any form or by any means—electronic, mechanical, photocopy, recording, or by any information storage and retrieval system—except for the inclusion of brief quotations in a review, without written permission from the author. Internet addresses (URLs) in this book were valid at the time of publication. However, the author is not responsible for missing or changed addresses.

Unless otherwise indicated, Scripture quotations are from the *New King James Version*. ©1982 by Thomas Nelson, Inc. Used by permission. All rights reserved.

Scripture quotations are from the *New American Standard Bible*, © 1975 by the Lockman Foundation Co. Used by permission.

Scripture quotations are from the Holy Bible, *New International Version*, ©1991 by International Bible Society. Used by permission of Zondervan Publishing House.

ISBN: 978-0-9820982-2-6

Printed in the United States of America

Victory Won Publications—Mission Statement
We are committed to publishing books that share a clear gospel of Jesus Christ, and that edify and encourage believers in their Christian walk.

Disclaimer

While this guide offers many answers and suggestions, it does not and cannot cover all possibilities or situations. It does not and cannot provide answers to all questions regarding dating and marriage. This book represents a biblical perspective of God's standards and applies them to dating. The author's opinions reflect her biblical mindset of what would be honoring to the Lord.

Contents

1. Singles, What Does God Want from You? 5
2. Why Planning a Marriage Is Important for Its Success . . . 16
3. How Prepared Are You for Marriage? 30
4. Is There Something Better Than Modern Dating? 48
5. Do You Know Important Principles for Spouse Selection? . 56
6. How to Avoid Infatuation Mistakes 66
7. What Is a Proper Friendship? 79
8. Do You Have Dating Discernment? 87
9. How to Be Faithful to Your Future Spouse 98
10. What You Need to Know about Flirting 110
11. Modesty: How Much Are You Compromising? 116
12. What You Need to Know to Avoid Sexual Temptation . . 136
13. What You Need to Know about Bonding 149
14. Happily Single—How to Have Ultimate Peace 160
15. Glossary 175
16. Recommended Reading 178
17. Audio Resources 179
18. About the Author 180

Introduction

About What Do Singles Worry?

- ♥ Jack, almost 32, doubts he will ever find a Christian woman to marry. "I want to rely on God, but I'm having a difficult time," he admits.

- ♥ Emma writes, "I am 28 years old, never married, and a Christian for two years. Since I have lived more time as unsaved than as a Christian, I wonder what the Bible says about dating."

- ♥ "What's so wrong with dating an unsaved person? Can't I just date and have fun?" asks Christine.

- ♥ Hunter writes, "In my youth, I was morally impure, but for years I have remained sexually pure. What advice or comments do you have for me?'

- ♥ Nick asks, "How will I know when I meet the right one? How can I prepare for marriage while I date?"

Besides addressing those concerns, this biblically based guide will:

- √ Encourage believers to trust God in finding a mate while presenting principled guidelines for selecting a lifelong spouse.

- √ Provide biblical tactics for following God's will for sexual purity before marriage.

√ Demonstrate several ways to remain faithful to a future spouse.

√ Offer recommendations for marriage preparation including biblical principles for a satisfied, thriving marriage.

√ Reveal why the threefold design for marriage remains the prevailing conduct for principled dating.

√ Examine how to be happily single and what pleases God in singlehood.

Note: This book includes true-to-life illustrations with names changed to protect privacy. Quotes identified as CBZ are from *The Complete Book of Zingers*.

Book Overview
A unique feature of this book is its foundation on the gospel of Christ, which is the basis for all Christian living. Therefore, the biblical wisdom in this guide will aid the single in making a wise mate selection and thus increase the chances of marital success. The essential biblical principles and insights for marriage included here provide the reader with keys to a satisfying marriage. This guidebook also provides information for avoiding the heartbreaks and dangers of modern dating.

This manual provides educational information for:

➤ Those dating or planning to date.

➤ Study and discussion groups including Christian high school juniors and seniors.

➤ Parents interested in preparing their preteen and teens for post-high school dating. The suggested parental guidance age for teen reading is 15 years old or higher, but parental involvement with discussion is advised.

➤ Pastors and youth group leaders.

Who Will Benefit Most from This Guide?

Written for believers in Jesus Christ, this book presents a biblical perspective; therefore, believers will gain the most from it. You can't base relationships on Christ if you don't know Him. Do you have a personal relationship with Jesus Christ? Do you know for sure you will spend eternity in heaven?

This is how God saves people. Since all people are sinners (Romans 3:23), a sinless God cannot have sinners live with Him in heaven. The penalty for sin is death (separation) from God in the terrors of hell forever. Sinners must pay for their sins unless there is a substitute, which there is. In His unlimited love, God the Father sent Christ—the God-Man—to earth to be the substitute. Paul writes, *"that Christ died for our sins according to the Scriptures and that He was buried, and that He rose again the third day according to the Scriptures, and that He was seen by Cephas, then by the twelve"* (1 Corinthians 15:3-5).

God poured out His wrath on Christ as punishment for the sins of the entire world. *"For God so loved the world that He gave His only begotten Son, that whoever believes in Him should not perish but have everlasting life"* (John 3:16). Believe that Christ took your punishment; God saves you and gives you eternal life.

To add anything—good behavior, good works, church attendance, baptism, or other church traditions or rituals (man's rules)—is the same as saying "Christ's work was not enough; I must add something." If you add to His work, you cancel God's work of grace for yourself and, therefore, you aren't saved. *"I do not set aside the grace of God, for if righteousness could be gained through the law [doing], Christ died for nothing!"* (Galatians 2:21 NIV).

Also, God declares *"And according to the Law, one may almost say, all things are cleansed with blood, and without shedding of blood there is no forgiveness"* (Hebrews 9:22 NASB). Is there shedding of blood with good behavior, good works, church attendance, baptism, or other church traditions or rituals? No, there isn't. So, there is no "forgiveness" of sin here. People relying on these things have no forgiveness; they remain lost. Only the blood sacrifice of Jesus Christ covers the payment for all sin. If you add to His work, you cancel out God's work of grace and, thus, you remain convicted of your sin. *"For by grace you have been saved through faith, and that not of yourselves; it is the gift of God, not of works, lest anyone should boast"* (Ephesians 2:8-9).

When a sinner believes in Christ's finished work, the Holy Spirit gives him eternal life with God. A believer can never lose eternal life—once saved always saved—because salvation is the work of God. *"And I give them eternal life, and they shall never perish; neither shall anyone snatch them out of My hand"* (John 10:28). No one can undo God's work!

CHAPTER 1

Singles, What Does God Want from You?

Have you experienced a broken heart?
How do you see yourself as a single?
How does God want you to spend your time?
What is the main emphasis of the Christian life, even dating?

This chapter will:

- ♥ Help you cope with a broken heart.

- ♥ Review our Father's perception of you.

- ♥ Provide guidelines for redeeming the time.

- ♥ Emphasize the objective of the Christian life.

- ♥ Encourage you to be happily single.

Have You Experienced a Broken Heart?

Many people believe the lie that suffering emotional pain and hurt is a normal part of dating. Imagine that after years of dating upheaval with 5 to 10 dating partners (more or less), you now meet the right person. But because you fear rejection again, you can't trust, you are unfriendly, and you are unapproachable. You protect yourself mentally and emotionally by withdrawing from future associations.

Distorted modern dating produces emotional upheaval of hurt feelings, sadness, grief, anger, self-doubt, and mistrust that repeat with each breakup. Besides the pain, dating break-ups create mistrust that carries over into marriage. This pattern of connecting and breaking up can also become a practice for divorce.

How Can We Encourage Someone Who Has Broken Up?
Don't offer useless, discouraging comments such as "he was no good" or "she had too many problems." Instead, give them information on how to avoid the pain of modern dating altogether as discussed in this book.

When down in the mouth, remember Jonah.
He came out all right!
—Thomas Edison

Individuals with broken hearts can harbor their hurt as well as develop bitterness, hatred, and anger, which grieves the Holy Spirit (Ephesians 4:30-31). Harboring those emotions not only hinder your spiritual life, but they can make you ill. Perhaps you feel far from God as a result but wish to draw closer to the Lord. You can get as close to God as you want—draw near to Him, and He will draw near to Him (James 4:8). Draw near in prayer, telling Him about your broken heart and spend time in His Word. Our Lord understands what we experience. *"The LORD is close to the brokenhearted and saves those who are crushed in spirit"* (Psalm 34:18 NIV). Let your painful experience draw you closer to your Savior.

Instead of rehearsing your disappointments,
enrich your mind with God's truths and promises.

How Do People Perceive You?

What do people see when they observe you or hear you speak? Can they notice that you feel sorry for yourself because you're not married or engaged like your friends? Does your face reveal that you are an unhappy single? Being self-absorbed and focused on finding a spouse isn't attractive to anyone. The following quotation offers encouragement to find everything in Christ.

> "The just shall live by faith," not only in your circumstances but in everything. I believe the Lord allows many things to happen on purpose to make us feel our need of Him. The more you find Him in your sorrows or wants, the more you will be attached to Him and drawn away from the place where the sorrows are, to Him in the place where He is.
> —J. B. Stoney, quoted in Miles Stanford's, *Position Papers* (out of print).

Happily Single

When asked if she was married,
Patty replied, "I'm an unclaimed treasure!"

Patty stated a truth but let's reflect on additional truth. Dear believer, your Savior treasures you! The God of the universe cherishes you because He sees you joined forever in His Son. When you grasp the great value God places on you, you won't feel abandoned by God or have feelings of low self-worth because you are single. When you slip into self-pity and think no one loves you, it is time to stop and think about His precious promises. *"But God demonstrates his own love for us in this: While we were still sinners, Christ died for us"* (Romans 5:8 NIV). Or, think about the love from your Best Friend. *"Greater love has no one than this, than to lay down one's life for his friends"* (John 15:13). *"As the Father has loved me, so have I loved you. Now remain in my love"* (John 15:9 NIV). Why feel discouraged when Christ treasures you?

How to Be a Contented Single

Adapted from "Contentment in Singleness" by Lydia M. Erb. Originally written about contentment for women, but is modified here to include men.

"If only I were married, I'd be happy!" When I hear someone say that I feel like asking," Why aren't you happy now?" A person who is unhappy or discontented as a single person is not apt to find that marriage would live up to her expectations.

The problem is the trait of self-centeredness. Individuals should not desire marriage to have someone to cater to their needs or desires. Instead, she should be thinking of whether she could enrich the life of her husband if the Lord would grant one. Instead of feeling that his virtues go unnoticed, his concerns should be about letting the Lord make him into the person who would be a desirable partner for a worthy woman. A discontented man or woman will not encourage friendship, nor would someone want to know an unhappy person better.

Contentment is a matter of choice. The apostle Paul states, *"I have learned in whatsoever state I am, in addition to that to be content"* (Philippians 4:11b). Paul was in jail when he wrote that! Contentment can be learned, regardless of the circumstances. First Timothy 6:6 reminds us, *"But godliness with contentment is great gain."* Whether married or single, our relationship to the Lord Jesus Christ is the key to finding satisfaction in life. When we find our joy in a close walk with the Lord, whether we are married or single doesn't matter.

I can speak from "both sides of the fence." I was content being single. Although I wasn't looking for a husband, when I was 26 years old the Lord brought me one. After 21 years of a satisfying marriage, the Lord took my partner Home—I was single again. I've spent more years being single than married, before and after marriage. It has been my experience that as long as the Lord Jesus Christ is central in a person's life, the single person can be just as joyful, contented, and fulfilled as those married. I do not envy those happily married, and when I see or hear of those who have marital problems, I'm glad that I'm single! "It's better to *be* single than to wish you were!" Too many people could verify that saying!

Although a successful marriage has its advantages, so does a single life. It's simpler for an unmarried person to spend time in prayer and God's Word than someone with a spouse and family. With fewer responsibilities, there's freedom to help with local church activities, to be available for counseling, for extending hospitality, and for fulfilling a prayer ministry. In our busy, modern age, we need much prayer. We should pray for our missionaries, our brothers, and sisters in Christ, the unsaved around the world, our homes, our nation, ourselves; the list is endless. Scripture commands in Ephesians 5:16 to *"Redeem the time because the days are evil."* Certainly, if we look around for opportunities to serve, there is no room for boredom.

Whether married or single, we can discover blessings in the common things of life. Do we take time to enjoy a beautiful sunrise or sunset, the songs of the birds, or the chorus of the frogs in spring, the loveliness or fragrance of the flowers in bloom? Do we take God's creation for granted without appreciating it? Are we thankful for our senses to enjoy all the Lord has provided? How we react makes a difference in our view of life in general.

We can develop a thankful view of blessings, great or small. If we grumble or complain because of what we don't have, we are ungrateful, which is a sin. In Romans, chapter 1, we read of the seriousness of sin. Verse 21 states, *"Because, although they knew God, they glorified Him not as God, nor were thankful."* The rest of the chapter describes the gross sins that followed. Ingratitude implies that we don't trust what God does for us is best. We think that *if* we had *our* way, we could do a better job of ordering our lives than God does! In Psalm 84:11b, the psalmist wrote, *"No good thing will He withhold from them that walk uprightly."* Do we believe that? If we do, we can be content with our place in life.

The little chorus, J-O-Y (Jesus, Others, and You), has a practical message. If you put Jesus first, others second, and yourself last, you will have real *joy*. Most people put themselves first, so is it any wonder that they missed God's best?

If you are still without a life partner, patiently wait for the Lord with the assurance that His plans are always best. His timing is perfect. Therefore, cheerful acceptance of the Lord's will for your life can be reflected in everything you do. Is it His will for you to have a spouse? If so, in His time He will provide one for you. Is it His will for you to remain single? If so, accept the challenge gracefully, making the most of opportunities singlehood offers to serve Him. (Having a "pity party" won't help!). In either case, Philippians 4:4 reminds us, *"Rejoice in the Lord always, and again I say, Rejoice!"* You *can* rejoice if you *will*. The choice is yours.

You can be happily single in the Lord!

How Would God Have You Make the Most of Your Time?

The Lord through the apostle Paul has the answer for you. *"Be very careful, then, how you live—not as unwise but as wise, making the most of every opportunity* [redeeming the time], *because the days are evil. Therefore do not be foolish, but understand what the Lord's will is"* (Ephesians 5:15-17 NIV). According to this verse, we should make the most of our lives and use our gifts and talents to serve Him and others.

Faithfulness in the ordinary tasks prepares individuals for greater responsibilities such as household duties or everyday jobs. Remember

Rebecca in the Old Testament (Genesis 24), who faithfully fulfilled her daily duties. Since Rebecca was faithful to her chores, she went to the well to draw water for her family. At the well, she met Abraham's servant—the connection to her future husband. Because she was faithful in her responsibilities, she kept the divine appointment that God in His wisdom planned for her. If you are a sensible believer, look at your responsibilities and relationships as opportunities that God can use, according to His plan and purpose, for your future.

As a Christian, you always represent Christ, therefore; *"Walk in wisdom toward those who are outside, redeeming the time"* (Colossians 4:5). When we obey the command to "redeem the time," not only are we using our time sensibly, but we are also preparing for the next stage of life, which may be marriage.

Redeeming the Time in Relationships

Singlehood can be a time to serve others and develop relationships. As a single person, use every opportunity to serve other members of your family and bond with them. Spending time with family members individually and collectively helps you know them on a deeper level. If possible, read Scripture and pray with them. Singleness can be a time to practice communicating intelligently and effectively with members of your family. Also, instead of withdrawing when a problem arises, practice resolving problems through effective communication.

> *"Let your speech always be gracious, seasoned with salt,*
> *so that you may know how you ought to answer*
> *everyone"* (Colossians 4:6 NRSV).

Demonstrate *agape* love—doing what is best for another in light of eternity, despite the personal cost to you. *Agape* love includes a servant's approach towards family members and prepares you for marriage. Loving and serving others as unto the Lord is the objective, not merely practicing on them. A man who demonstrates love, respect, and protection for his mother and sisters (for all women) prepares for godly behavior towards a future wife. Ladies, view your relationships with your father as a training ground for respecting your future husband. Interaction with family members contributes to the development of your qualities and outlook, which can benefit future relationships.

Redeeming the Time with Christ

A Christ-focused life is the best gift you can offer Christ and a future spouse. Making Christ the focus of your life and living by faith will prepare you for the future. As the pattern of Christ-centered dependency becomes your standard, shifting your thoughts back to Christ and His promises becomes easier. Your spiritual life and growth are essential to your Christian life and a future spouse.

> *Two things mark spiritual growth:*
> *one is a deeper sense of the sinful old nature;*
> *the other is a greater longing after the Lord Jesus Christ.*
> —J.B. Stoney

Besides dependency on Him and trusting His promises, what else does God desire from you? Your Father wants the abundant life for you regardless of your status—married or single. How? Through faith, the Spirit of God produces *in you* the abundant life—the Life of Christ, also called the fruit of the Spirit. Depending on your development, singleness is a time to mature emotionally and spiritually. Singleness is a time to allow the Holy Spirit to conform you into the likeness of Christ (Romans 8:29; 12:2; 2 Corinthians 3:18).

> *God's purpose is not to make us comfortable*
> *but conformable—conformable to Christ.*
> —*The Complete Book of Zingers* (CBZ)

Since our heavenly Father wants us to hold Him accountable for His promises, we can pray back to Him the following Colossian verses describing a life of faith.

For this reason, since the day we heard about you, we have not stopped praying for you and asking God to fill you with the knowledge of his will through all spiritual wisdom and understanding.

[10] And we pray this in order that you may live a life worthy of the Lord and may please him in every way: bearing fruit in every good work, growing in the knowledge of God,

[11] being strengthened with all power according to his glorious might so that you may have great endurance and patience, and joyfully understanding.

[12] giving thanks to the Father, who has qualified you to share in the inheritance of the saints in the kingdom of light.

[13] For he has rescued us from the dominion of darkness and brought us into the kingdom of the Son he loves,

[14] in whom we have redemption, the forgiveness of sins.

—Colossians 1:9-14 NIV)

As you yield to Him, He blesses you with the abundant life, and Christ receives the glory.

> The heart that is hungry to have God's purpose worked out in his life is going to be neither disappointed nor pampered. When it comes to seeing self for what it is, there can be no pampering; when it comes to seeing the Lord Jesus Christ for who He is, there can be no disappointment.
> —Miles J. Stanford,
> *None But The Hungry Heart*, 4-24.

How Can You Treasure Your Spiritual Bridegroom?

How should a single person respond to Christ, the real love of the believer's life? If you want the best life, put all your trust in God, reject your limited viewpoint, and honor Him in every area of your life. *"Trust in the LORD with all your heart, And lean not on your own understanding; In all your ways acknowledge Him, And He shall direct your paths"* (Proverbs 3:5-6). The key to a godly heart is submitting to the Lord's direction, knowing that He has the best answers to every need and is faithful to provide His best (Philippians 4:19).

Ponder this compelling quote, which reflects your relationship with Jesus Christ, your Spiritual Bridegroom.

> His love is mine when I know what He did for me; my love is His when I know who He is to me—He who is Love is my Life. He loved and died that I might live, and love. The Lord wins my heart in His humiliation; He satisfies it in His glory. A won heart is not necessarily a satisfied heart. But if a heart is truly won by the Lord Jesus, it never will be satisfied without Him. No heart that is won is ever satisfied but in the company of the One who won it. Absence does not 'make the heart grow fonder'! You only discover in absence what you have gained in presence.
>
> —Miles Stanford,
> *None But the Hungry Heart*, 7-19.

Living for Christ satisfies all your needs and longings.

Study Questions

Give Scripture verses when you can.

1. After a breakup, how could you comfort yourself or another using God's Word?

2. What have you learned or reviewed about contentment after reading this chapter?

3. How will you redeem the time in relationships?

4. How will you redeem the time with Christ?

5. From this chapter, what can you apply to your life?

CHAPTER 2

Why Planning a Marriage Is Important for Its Success

Why would you like to marry?
Are your friends engaged or getting married?
Is love enough to sustain a life-long marriage?

In this chapter we will:

- ♥ Discover why planning a wedding isn't as important as you may think.

- ♥ Learn why love isn't enough.

- ♥ Inspect God's design and perspectives on marriage.

- ♥ Link the importance of God's design for marriage with selective dating.

Why Is Planning a Wedding Not so Important?

Typically, couples spend too much time planning expensive weddings, and people pour more time and effort into an impressive wedding celebration than the marriage preparation. Many brides dream of a Pinterest or Facebook wedding production to show the world. Extravagant weddings are costly and often beyond your budget, which is not good stewardship. If the great event overrides the marriage focus, an emotional let down may occur afterward.

If the couple planned a simpler wedding, it would be easier to keep the focus on the future marriage. The wedding ceremony is an opportunity to share the gospel of Jesus Christ and can include how the couple came to know Christ and then each other. Wedding receptions can be fun parties especially when family and friends are involved in the preparations. Working together on the preparations encourages bonding and generates memories between families. It is also more economical— minimizes or eliminates debt.

Wedding celebrations last several hours, but a marriage lasts a lifetime (or should). Two important considerations are: 1) How much time should I spend thinking and preparing for marriage? 2) How much should we spend on the wedding so we won't have debt, which could be harmful to our marriage?

Before you consider marriage, a clear understanding of God's design and purpose for marriage is essential, which this chapter discusses.

Let's consider a few reasons the following couples wanted to marry.

- ♥ Convinced that Deanna would make him happy, Kurt wanted to marry her. All his friends were married, and he wanted to fit in.

- ♥ Since Cindy and Zach loved each other, they decided to marry, raise a family, and serve the Lord.

- ♥ Lonely Becky eagerly anticipated marrying Jack because she supposed he would rescue her from her unhappy home life. She wanted to escape her domineering, disapproving mother and abusive alcoholic father so she could be happy.

Happiness, Is That All There Is?

Many people think that marriage will make them happy and dream of living happily ever after. Happiness is a feeling based on experiences or circumstances. The two forms of happiness produce feelings of satisfaction, but each lasts a different span of time. First, the feel-good happiness is a momentary sensation of pleasure. For example, when we hear a funny story, or when someone compliments us for some accomplishment, we experience feel-good happiness. Feel-good happiness rarely lasts longer than a few minutes or a few hours at most.

In comparison, value-based happiness is a deeper emotion from a life that has meaning. Because value-based happiness is a source of satisfaction, it is long lasting. We enjoy value-based happiness from faithfulness and diligence while working on a job, earning a degree, or completing education or training.

How to Have Something Greater Than Human Happiness

All of us have a natural emptiness in their soul, which we try to fill with something or someone to make us happy. Countless Christians have discovered something greater than happiness—genuine joy. We can experience this joy despite our greatest troubles. Abraham, David, and Paul found joy, as have millions of others. You can experience peace too.

While happiness depends on circumstances and is temporary, joy depends on our relationship with the Lord Jesus. Because our joy (inner contentment) occurs from our unique association—our union with our Savior—it lasts. When we consider the qualities of our God—love, faithfulness, grace, and countless others, we can have joy, regardless of the circumstances (Nehemiah 8:10). Instead of focusing on our circumstances, we can choose to reflect on our Savior—His person and His work. Joy comes from dwelling on the truth of His Word and His promises. Joy in Him occurs when we reflect on His plan for our life (Jeremiah 29:11; Romans 8:29) and His even-better plan for our eternal life with Him (1 Peter 1:3-5).

Unless we fill the God-shaped void in our soul with Christ, we will never experience contentment—His joy. We will keep looking for that "something" or "someone" to fill the God-void.

Jesus is the gift that perfectly fits the size of every heart.

What Are Poor Reasons to Get Married?

- ♥ Happiness is the dominant motive.
- ♥ Loneliness
- ♥ Status—all my friends are married.
- ♥ A sense of belonging
- ♥ Escape from a troublesome home or family life
- ♥ Security—financial

Did you notice that the reasons listed above focus on self?

Take a few moments to consider the following:

- √ What benefits will you gain from marrying?
- √ What will you contribute to the marriage?
- √ Are you looking for companionship or want to have a family or both?

Consider God-Pleasing Reasons to Marry

Although we never marry to be unhappy, happiness isn't the final goal in marriage. However, satisfaction in marriage can result from the following reasons for marrying. Notice the emphasis on service, not selfishness, in these reasons.

- ♥ The man: to love and protect her

- ♥ The woman: to respect and be a help to him

- ♥ To demonstrate unconditional, sacrificial love; to serve each other

- ♥ To start a family

- ♥ Companionship

> *Love has nothing to do with what you are expecting*
> *to get—only with what you are expecting to give,*
> *which is everything.*
> —Katherine Hepburn

When Love Is Not a Reason to Marry

Avoid marrying just because you love someone. Although a Christian couple may love each other, for various reasons, they choose not to marry. To love and marry a drug addict, an alcoholic, a lazy person, or a dependent or needy person can be disastrous to your future and that of any children you may have. Marrying someone who has serious flaws because you love him is a risky decision. Thinking you can change someone is foolish since no one can stop unhealthy, negative behavior. Changes must come from within a person.

Marrying for Love May Be out of God's Will

For example, God forbids marrying an unsaved person. Even if you think you could lead the person to Christ, God forbids becoming connected unequally. Forsaking the love of your life because the person rejects Jesus Christ may be a difficult decision, but God honors those who chose to follow His will.

> *True freedom is not having our own way*
> *but yielding to God's way.*
>
> —CBZ

Following God's Will Is Always Best

Scripture speaks of numerous people who made the right decision and followed God's will regardless of their cost or risk. For example, Esther risked her life to see the king (her husband) without his invitation. Her objective was saving the Jews (her people) from extermination, and God honored her obedience. Because Jesus Christ left the comforts of heaven to obey His Father's will and died on Calvary's cross, God the Father honored Him and blessed us.

Communication with the Lord via prayer allows Him to counsel us with His wisdom through His Word. Since God loves you with unfathomable love, He sets moral standards of behavior to protect you. Foolish decisions that disregard God's will cause us to forfeit His blessings and suffer His divine discipline.

> *Many pray not to find God's will,*
> *but to get his approval of their own.*
> *Don't expect God's approval of plans*
> *on which he has not been consulted.*
>
> —CBZ

Why God's Perspective on Marriage Is Fundamental

The Christian life begins with your thinking. Since thinking precedes feelings and behaviors, we should think from God's viewpoint in the Christian life and marriage. Understanding God's perspective on marriage is fundamental to marriage success.

1. **What Is God's Plan for the Christian Marriage?**
   God instituted marriage, which He details in His Word. God's plan for marriage is universal—one man and one woman as genetically defined—committed for life. Since He designed marriage, His plan is for *all* married couples, whether living under the same roof or living a continent apart. However, the definitive key to a thriving marriage requires making Christ the hub, followed by Christ-centered living. The relationship between a believing husband and wife should illustrate the love that exists between Christ, the Bridegroom and the Church, His bride (Matthew 25:1-13; Revelation 19:7-8, 21:2). Successful marriage and family life revolve around Jesus Christ—the only source of contentment and fulfillment.

2. **What Are Important Responsibilities Regarding Marriage?**
   God presented marriage as a gift to Adam and Eve. In His wisdom, God created them for each other. In marriage, the man and woman take responsibility for each other's welfare and commit to loving their spouse above all others (Genesis 2:18-24; Ephesians 5:22-33). He didn't create marriage just for convenience, but for a purpose.

3. **What Is God's Ultimate Purpose for Marriage?**
   God *did not* design marriage for individuals to seek happiness or self-gratification. Rather, He designed marriage as a place to serve one another in love, just as Christ served the Church and gave Himself for it (Ephesians 5).

*Marriage is for the glory of God our Father,
to model Christ's love and commitment to our spouses
and children, and to reveal Christ to the world.*

4. What are God's perfect principles for marriage?

God Desires that You Marry a Christian
*"Do not be unequally yoked together with unbelievers.
For what fellowship has righteousness with lawlessness?
And what communion has light with darkness?"*
(2 Corinthians 6:14).

God Designed Marriage To Be Permanent
*"So then, they are no longer two but one flesh. Therefore
what God has joined together, let not man separate"*
(Matthew19:6; also, Mark 10:1-12; Matthew 19:1-12).

Commitment Is Essential to a Successful Marriage
Genesis 24:58-60 illustrates the commitment Rebecca made to marry Isaac and to serve him. Commitment to each other serves to solidify a union.

How Can Your Marriage Be a Picture of Christ and His Church?

God intended marriage to serve as a picture or representation of the union between Christ and His Bride, the Church. Christ loved His Bride and gave Himself for her, and He commands that we *agape* love each other in the same way.

Christ demonstrated *agape* love throughout His earthly life. In sacrificial, *agape* love, Christ offered His life at Calvary to fulfill our need for redemption. Christ's love—*agape*—isn't a feeling but a mindset of choice, of action while depending upon His Father. Christ's submissiveness and obedience to His Father's will is another example of His love for us.

Agape **love is doing what's best for another in light of eternity despite the personal cost to you.** If both husband and wife follow Christ's example of *agape* love, submission and obedience to God, and they desire to serve each other, joy and satisfaction in marriage will reign.

In contrast to human love that any person can express, *agape* love is an action. The Spirit of God produces Christ's *agape* love through the believer in fellowship with God, that is, it is a mindset of choice while trusting God.

Understanding Love and Respect in Marriage

In preparation for marriage, individuals should understand another basic truth about husbands and wives. Wives and husbands seek different needs from each other.

What Does a Husband or a Wife Want More—Love or Respect?
While both are important, respect is more important to a man and love is more important to a woman. Why is that? God made the man with a strong need for respect, and He made women with a deeper need for love. Why else would God command, *"Let each one of you love his wife as himself, and let the wife see that she respects her husband"* (Ephesians 5:33).

God commands that wives submit (respect his authority) to their husbands as the final authority in the home and that husbands love their wives. A wife who yields to her husband's authority shows respect to him. *"Wives, submit to your husbands, as to the Lord. For the husband is the head of the wife as Christ is the head of the church, his body, of which he is the Savior"* (Ephesians 5:21-23 NIV).

Too many couples enter marriage unaware of this fundamental difference concerning love and respect between a husband and a wife. A bride confided that she and her husband often argued about his decisions, and she said things she regretted. Her grandma told her that if she thinks before she speaks, she won't need to offer apologies as often. Thinking before speaking shows respect to her husband as does allowing him to lead. Someone gave the couple Dr. Emerson Eggerichs' book, *Love & Respect.* The book showed the bride how to respect her husband, which resulted in her husband displaying more love to her in return. Dr. Eggerichs' *Love & Respect* is just the right "prescription" to cure marriage ills or better yet prevent them.

How Could You Show Unconditional Respect or Unconditional Love?

Husbands wonder how they can unconditionally love when wives fail them. Most wives want to show respect to their husbands, but they often don't understand how to do that. What a wife may think is respectful frequently differs from what a man needs to feel respected.

God commands a husband to *love* his wife unconditionally even if she doesn't respect him. Similarly, the Lord commands a wife to *respect* her husband unconditionally, even if he doesn't obey the command to love. In other words, a husband should *unconditionally love* a disrespectful wife and a wife should *unconditionally respect* an unloving husband. Therefore, practice *agape* love—*doing* what is best for another in light of eternity, despite the personal cost to you. *Agape* love is unconditional and sacrificial love.

Unconditional respect and unconditional love have *forgiveness* in common. Wives and husbands must remember that they are sinners, yet God forgives them unconditionally. God commands that a wife should unconditionally respect her husband even when he displays pride or harshness, or sins in other ways. But how? A wife's first response is recalling that she also sins daily, yet the Lord always forgives her. Since God doesn't hold our sin against us, we shouldn't seek revenge through silence or withholding kindness. An unforgiving believer is in a state of sin—out of fellowship and thus without God's blessing.

When our thinking aligns with God's, spouses realize that forgiving a spouse isn't optional but rather commanded by God. Thinking God's principles helps spouses feel compassion toward their spouses, who also struggle with sin. *"Be kind and compassionate to one another, forgiving each other, just as in Christ God forgave you"* (Ephesians 4:32 NIV). Because of your position in Christ, God forgives you unconditionally, and He commands you to forgive others unreservedly.

*Never stop forgiving others
until God stops forgiving you.*

Why Is Respect Most Important to a Husband?

A husband wants respect for who he is, rather than based on his performance. Studies show that respect is the number one need of most men. A survey of men helps us understand why respect is more important to a man than love. Some findings include:

- ♥ Respect from a wife expresses her trust in him. Trust comes before respect.

- ♥ Respect gives a husband the confidence that he can overcome challenges, that he can do difficult things. A wife's respect decreases his fear of inadequacy or failure.

- ♥ Respect recognizes his leadership and encourages involvement. Giving him respect helps him believe he can be the leader in the marriage (Ephesians 5:25-30).

- ♥ Respect offers encouragement that makes the husband want to display more love. If a wife doesn't respect her husband enough to listen to him, he will suffer defeat. If she shows respect by listening, he wants to love her even more.

Therefore, while you are dating, display *agape* love, which includes respect for each other. Women, in your words and deeds, express respect to him. Men and women, let your words and behavior reflect your Savior. *"Therefore, whether you eat or drink, or whatever you do, do all to the glory of God"* (1 Corinthians 10:31).

How Important Is a Marriage Mindset During Spouse Selection?

Because marriage is an important decision of your life, you must consider it seriously, beginning with the first date. A dating couple ought to remember God's design and plan for marriage. Follow God's model for marriage, which encompasses three essentials of Christian living:

1. **A Christ-focused perspective**
   Never underestimate the importance of making Christ your priority. Being Christ-centered is the best gift a Christian man can give his spouse. In Christ, we see a wonderful blending of strength and tenderness, and that's what it takes to be a godly husband. Although Sarah wasn't perfect, Peter points to her as a model for Christian wives to follow (1 Peter 3:6). Unless couples put Christ first and yield to God's will, they can't follow His example of love and service in their marriage.

   A personal relationship with Jesus Christ not only gives meaning to every facet of life, but it's the cornerstone of the Christian marriage. A thriving marriage takes three: the husband, the wife, and Jesus Christ in the spotlight.

   Put Christ in the center, and
   everything else comes together.

2. ***Agape* love**
   A satisfying marriage exhibits Christ's *agape* love—doing what is best for another in light of eternity, despite the

personal cost to you. *Agape* love includes the love & respect connection and guarantees a contented marriage.

> *Agape love is like cement—it holds a marriage together.*

3. **A mindset of serving one another as unto the Lord**
   Displaying *agape* love during dating includes a mindset of service. A growing believer places Christ first, and by faith allows His love to flow through him or her towards others. Service is love in action. Instead of seeking to serve, many couples, including Christians, marry to fulfill their needs. They want another to serve them instead of seeking to serve each other as Christ serves us, His Bride.

> *Some folks are poor spellers.*
> *They think "service" is spelled "serve us."*
> —R.C. Cunningham

In conclusion, we have examined the importance of understanding God's design, purpose, and perspectives on marriage. A couple needs to keep God's marriage design in mind while they are selectively dating. Couples who apply the three essentials of Christian living—a Christ-focused perspective, *agape* love, and a mindset of serving one another as unto the Lord—increase their success of finding a godly spouse. Just as planning for marriage should take more time and effort than planning a wedding celebration, a wise couple will give selective dating the time and commitment it deserves.

Study Questions

Cite Scripture verses when possible.

1. What is greater than happiness in marriage?

2. List five God-pleasing reasons to marry.

3. Give reasons when "love" isn't a reason to marry.

4. What is the key to a thriving marriage?

5. What is God's ultimate purpose for marriage?

6. What are God's principles for marriage?

7. Name the ways marriage should model Christ and His bride, the Church.

8. Explain how forgiveness is fundamental for unconditional love and unconditional respect. Give examples.

9. What does a husband want more than love? In a marriage, what does a wife desire most?

10. What are some principles of love and respect in marriage?

11. Wedding vows often include the vow to promise to love one another. But God exhorts a couple, *"Let each one of you love his wife as himself, and let the wife see that she respects her husband"* (Ephesians 5:33). Why would it be wise to include respect in the wedding vows of the wife?

12. What would be a godly mindset while dating?

CHAPTER 3

How Prepared Are You for Marriage?

Are your marriage expectations unrealistic?
How do you know if you are ready to selectively date?
How will you know when you're ready to commit to marriage?

In this chapter you will:

- ♥ Examine unrealistic expectations.

- ♥ Learn when to begin principled dating.

- ♥ Determine whether you are ready for marriage.

- ♥ Discover what influences dating conduct has on marriage.

Do You Have Unrealistic Marriage Expectations?

Some people have acquired unrealistic marriage expectations, which are one major cause of a failed marriage. Unless we replace them with the reality of day-to-day married life, these idealistic views may be roots for divorce. Some examples of unrealistic marriage expectations are listed below.

Marriage will make me happy. Marriage can sometimes make you unhappy, and that's normal. Believing that their spouse determines his or her happiness can lead to a miserable marriage. Other individuals aren't responsible for our happiness—we are.

After the wedding celebrations, couples must face the reality that marriage is the work of building a life together. Many of the same activities you did as a single you now perform with or alongside your spouse. As a single, and now as a married person, you work a job, perform household chores and maintenance, shop for groceries, pay the bills, pause for meals, grow tired, and repeat the routine the next day. Some couples are disappointed, even depressed when the highs of dating, the fun, and excitement fade. Couples can rise above the mundane routines of busy living by connecting daily. Shared Bible and prayer time can uplift you, and focusing on the Lord brings joy. Working on the marriage includes regular times together (dates) away from the routine and spending time alone can refresh you.

The soul mate myth leads to disappointment. The concept of *soul mate*, originating in Greek mythology, continues as beliefs in many religions. Soul mate implies that personality traits and attitudes perfectly match that of another. This idea promotes the myth that finding your soul mate guarantees happiness. Realistic people believe in the possibility of more than one suitable mate, which is also a biblical concept. In contrast to religion, Christianity—a relationship with Jesus Christ, not a religion—never uses the term *soul mate* nor does it allude to it.

Some individuals believe they will find happiness when they marry. They believe, "If I find the right person to marry, then I'll be happy." To some degree, this is true. Marrying a suitable person will increase your chances of a happy marriage. Although marriage can make us happy, it is unlikely marriage will provide intense happiness for as long as we think it should.

Furthermore, forget about prince charming or the woman on a pedestal myths. All of us are flawed sinners (Romans 3:23). Do not expect your future husband's attention to remain the same as they did during dating or your future wife to give you undivided attention anytime you wish it (especially after the children arrive). He may not give you flowers, and she may not be an organized housekeeper. He may be messy or drop his clothes next to the hamper. She may not fold his laundry the way he likes.

Neither a wife nor a husband will always do what is best for the other or for the marriage. What you think is best may not be what your spouse thinks is best. Irritating behaviors, spousal failures, and other annoyances may cause you to wonder why you married your spouse. Don't sweat the small stuff! Instead, love, respect, and serve one another as unto the Lord.

The fear of change is unrealistic. Nothing in this life remains constant including people, relationships, or marriage. Realistic spouses understand and expect that spouses may change. However, if you select a mate based on important issues such as beliefs, values, and standards that coincide with your own, then changes in those areas are unlikely. Expecting marriage to stay the same, as it was when you first married, is unrealistic. Growing as a person, especially spiritual maturation is a good form of change. Consistency in your attitude of *agape* love and your mindset of serving each other is good, but stagnation is not.

Fear of change could be the result of a loss or a dating heartbreak. Perhaps you haven't resolved or accepted that loss through the grief process. Maybe your fear of change stems from a fear of losing control related to some past event. However, facing your fears will enable you to move forward.

Clinging to your unchanging Savior, Jesus Christ,
will give you strength and courage for living.

Don't cling to unrealistic expectations regarding conflict. During the dating experience, expect to have arguments; there will be arguments in marriage, too. Don't treat an argument as a crisis with an attitude of "it's all over now." Arguments, if handled appropriately, are normal experiences through which a marriage can grow. Effective communication, including listening and giving feedback, is essential to conflict resolution.

Arguments offer opportunities to share
your viewpoint calmly and to listen to
your spouse's perspective.

Do you have unrealistic expectations about love? Often, people don't realize that love varies depending on the relationship. Different or variations of love occur between parents and children, friend to friend, brother to sister, and husband and wife. Misunderstandings about the kinds of love may cause people to *feel* they have fallen out of love.

In time, one or both spouses may begin to feel like they don't love their spouse anymore. Wasn't marriage supposed to make them happy? If they aren't happy, they might also question, "was there something wrong with me?" Much of the romance has faded, and they wonder, "Did we make a mistake in marrying each other?"

A marriage relationship may cool off because of unmet expectations. The question becomes: what were you in love with—your fantasy spouse?" Or, as old song lyrics ask, were you "falling in love with love"?

For example, Troy had misunderstood the variations of love, but years later he had the opportunity to talk about that with his ex-wife, Terry. He expressed regrets about his misunderstandings regarding love. Troy explained that when their daughter was born, he had a special kind of love for her—overwhelming love for her. He wanted to care for her. He remembered that he wanted to protect her and he recalled that he would have given his life for her.

Troy told his ex-wife about the surge of emotions at the birth of his daughter, and that he compared those feelings with his feelings towards his wife. Troy realized that he didn't have the same feelings towards her. So, he concluded that he didn't love Terry and began *looking for love* in all the wrong places (affairs). Eventually, Troy and Terry divorced. Looking back, Troy admitted to Terry that he has many regrets regarding his part in the breakup of their marriage.

As we view marriage realistically, we will see changes. As the routine of married life sets in, the newness of being in love fades, causing you to think that perhaps you have fallen out of love. It is normal to question your emotions. However, don't equate love with excitement, fascination, or the newness of marriage. The longer you are together, the more comfortable you will become with your spouse, resulting in the diminishment of the *initial* excitement. This comfortable aspect, including predictability, is part of the good developmental process of marriage and establishment of a family unit. As time passes, spousal love changes into something deeper, broader, more stable, and mature—that is, a growing love. Falling in love is easy; growing in love takes determination and work.

In contrast to frail changing human love, *agape* love is a choice to *do* what is best for another, in light of eternity, regardless of the personal cost. *Agape* love is not a feeling but an action—labor.

> *The labor of agape love keeps a marriage alive and well.*

What Are Some Realistic Perspectives after Marriage

What Happens When the Novelty of Marriage Wears Off?

Usually, couples begin their marriage in a blissful state of happiness. After the honeymoon, and for some time after, marriage is a novelty. The romance of fresh adventures, new experiences, and interesting discoveries about each other fill their lives. In this stage of marriage, the couple considers themselves to be in love. This romance stage lasts for varying lengths of time, depending on the couple.

Research shows that the happiness boost from marriage lasts only about two years. Unfortunately, after two years, many people who haven't fulfilled their goal of finding the ideal partner are unhappy. Many of these individuals have the wrong perspective on marriage or married for the wrong reason. Individuals complain, "I'm not happy in this marriage. God wants me to be happy, so I want out of this marriage." A self-centered perspective confuses self-gratification with happiness. Pursuing pleasure at the cost of a meaningful relationship never works.

The Honeymoon Ended, But New Challenges and Growth Emerge
When the honeymoon stage fades into the routine reality of everyday living, other issues may arise. Low self-worth or neglect during childhood or youth often encourages unrealistic expectations from marriage. Happiness will be difficult to find if you base your worth on how others treat you. Our contentment must come from within, especially from our relationship with Jesus Christ, our source of genuine worth.

Rose struggled with low self-worth during her engagement and early years of marriage when the dating level of affection and attention faded. She shares,

> I believe it was the Lord's will that my husband and I married, which the Lord confirmed that in many ways. My struggle in our engagement period and early on in our marriage was evaluating my worth according to the way my husband responded to me. Early on, he showed so much affection and love. It was easy to feel special and valued. However, as we got busy with life, he wasn't as affectionate as he was previously.
>
> The Lord used these times to draw me closer to Him, and I discovered my value in Christ, my Savior. As Ephesians 2:4-7 expresses,
>
>> *But God, who is rich in mercy, because of His great love with which He loved us,[5] even when we were dead in trespasses, made us alive together with Christ (by grace you have been saved),[6] and raised us up together, and made us sit together in the heavenly places in Christ Jesus,[7] that in the ages to come He might show the exceeding riches of His grace in His kindness toward us in Christ Jesus.*
>
> From this experience, I learned that as a believer, I am in Christ. I am His child and dearly loved by God. I have Christ's

righteousness. I realized that I am of great value to God and that He has a specific plan and purpose for me.

The Benefits of Realistic Expectations

True biblical marriage is more than romantic ecstasy kindled through imagination. Marriage consists of a series of seasons from honeymoon to the empty nest and retirement. In each stage, a couple who irons out the wrinkles reaps the benefit in later years. For example, many young people have difficulty imagining that a white-haired grandma is more likely to have a deeper, stronger love for her bald, pot-bellied hubby watching TV than she ever imagined in their dating days. Feelings like these result from a life built together amid the difficult and good times, the tears and the joy. Hopefully, a couple will progress from romantic fireworks to deep, sustaining, genuine love and thriving lives of shared experiences and memories. The Christ-centered marriage can experience an even higher plane by growing together in the Lord.

> *Marriage is not a vacation or a picnic.*
> *Rather, marriage is a career that demands*
> *the very best of both partners.*
> *Marriage is a testing-ground for one's integrity,*
> *courage, and character.*
>
> —J. Allen Petersen,
> *Inspiring Quotations*

What Is the Right Age to Consider Marriage?

Common sense suggests dating later instead of sooner. Therefore, middle school children and teens shouldn't date; instead, let them complete their childhood. Frequently, the earlier a person dates, the earlier he or she marries, which may be too young. Rather than one-on-one dating, children and teens should enjoy each other's company in group settings and avoid adult dating activity.

Few high school sweethearts marry and have happy, successful marriages. The divorce rate for teens who marry at 16 or 17 doubles that of age 18 or 19. The divorce rate decreases slightly for those marrying in their late teens in contrast with those who marry in their 20s. The pressures of teen years, plus immaturity, and the stresses of married life increase the risk of divorce. Individuals need to take time to mature before taking on adult activities and responsibilities.

One study suggests that waiting until age 25 or older to marry is best. A University of Utah study in 2015 asserted an ideal age for a lasting marriage is between 28 and 32. This study further concluded the odds of divorce increasingly decline with age from the teen years through the twenties and early thirties. But this research also noted the chances of divorce increase as you move into the late thirties and early forties. After age 32, the divorce risk increases about five percent each year.

However, while these findings are noteworthy, they are merely statistics. Maturity and a willingness to sacrifice independence are more important than age. Marrying beyond age 25 brings challenges such as changing set habits. Many wisely postpone marriage until after college. Instead of focusing on the best age to marry, concentrate on personal maturation, plus growing in the Lord.

How Will You Know When to Date?

Just because you may want to marry doesn't mean you are ready. Before considering marriage, you must be ready to commit to making the marriage work. Therefore, maturity and knowing yourself are essential before you consider marriage.

Are You Ready for Marriage?

Questions to ask include:

- ♥ Am I spiritually growing in my faith and dependency on the Lord Jesus?

- ♥ Is my education or career training completed? (Ideally, this is best.)

- ♥ Men: Is my income enough to support a family?

- ♥ Am I willing to show *agape* love—choosing to do what is best for another in light of eternity, despite the personal cost to me? Am I able to love unconditionally and sacrificially?

- ♥ Do I have a mindset of service? Am I willing to give more than I receive or do I give to get? Will I give 100% unconditionally?

- ♥ Men: Am I mature enough to assume leadership of the household, especially the spiritual realm of marriage? A husband's leadership gives the wife a sense of security.

- ♥ Women: Am I ready to place myself under the authority and spiritual leadership of a husband?

- ♥ Women: Do you have basic domestic skills: cooking, cleaning, laundry, grocery shopping?

- ♥ Men: Do you have domestic skills to maintain the household if your spouse cannot?

- ♥ Do you have basic knowledge of home repairs, maintenance, and yard care?

- ♥ Men and women: Can I balance a checkbook, live within a budget, and manage my finances?

- ♥ Am I ready to yield much of my independence and assume the *us* approach?

- ♥ Am I mature emotionally, that is, able to understand and manage my emotions?

Indications of Emotional Maturity

Every individual has a specific degree of emotional maturity. With effort, each person's measure of maturity can improve. The following list will help you estimate your ranking of emotional maturity. However, no one can meet all of these points and perfection isn't the objective.

Flexibility. Can you see a circumstance as unique and adapt to it? When problems occur, can you identify how to respond next time? Can you suggest a plan for changes?

Responsibility. Do you take responsibility for your actions or do you blame others when problems arise? Do you understand that you are a product of your decisions, not your circumstances, past and present?

Problem-solving. Can you identify a problem and think of a solution, then research the best way to complete that solution? Are you willing to seek God's guidance?

Personal growth. Do you meet future challenges by gaining knowledge today that will help you in the future? Do you need to learn and plan that into your schedule?

Open-minded. Do you believe that sometimes better ways of handling problems or conflicts are available? Are you willing to seek opinions and views of others? Or, do you feel threatened when people disagree with you? Do you habitually become angry or pout when you don't get your way? If someone shows you a better way, can you happily do it that way?

Nonjudgmental. When you disagree with others, can you refrain from criticizing them? Are you willing to respect their right to their convictions?

Resilience. Life will always include circumstances that go wrong; expect setbacks and disappointments. Initially, you may be upset, but if you are emotionally mature, you will express your feelings, recognize actions you can take, and move forward.

A Calm Manner. No one can be calm 100 percent of the time, but a mature person displays composure most of the time. Or, is life always drama that seeks control by overreacting?

Realistic Optimism. You aren't deceived and believe that anything worthwhile requires effort and patience. Your optimistic nature based on God's principles causes you to believe you can manage, regardless of circumstances. In your optimism, when you have opportunities, you go after them.

Approachability. Since you're friendly and sociable, people feel comfortable around you, so you develop friendships easily. Can you trust the Lord to help you socialize despite your anxieties?

Confidence. You feel comfortable accepting the praise and compliments of others. You understand that you can't please everyone; some people will disapprove of you or what you do. You have convictions and act on them regardless of whether people agree or disagree.

Humor. When you are the target of a joke, can you laugh with friends or coworkers? You don't take yourself too seriously.

Teachable. Are you able to accept direction, criticism, or correction? Are you humble so you can be teachable?

Humility. Are you humble enough to say, "I was wrong" or "I don't know!" or "I'm sorry."

What personality traits positively influence you?
Sally writes,

> The traits of humility and being teachable attracted me to my husband because they made me feel safe enough to commit to him. A lack of confidence becomes a great obstacle to emotional maturity. However, confidence comes from developing the mind of Christ through the consistent intake and application of His word. In essence, confidence for the believer is confidence in Christ (John 15:4-5).

An emotionally mature person takes charge of her own life. He has a mental picture of life and has the ambition to fulfill dreams and goals. Emotional maturity produces a happy, healthy life and increases respect for others. Life becomes a delight instead of a duty to a mature person. Emotional development takes time, effort, and patience. Although childhood and teen years should be the training camp for maturity, some adult individuals remain immature.

*Maturity must come before
assuming adult responsibilities.*

Insightful Advice on Love from Solomon

This next section offers dating conduct that can positively affect your future marriage. While this isn't a detailed study of Song of Solomon, it highlights basic truths as applied to courtship. However, we will apply its biblical wisdom to principled dating, which follows biblical standards to keep in mind while dating.

In the Old Testament book, Song of Songs (also called "Song of Solomon"), God describes courtship, the wedding, and marriage. Song of Songs purposes to exalt human love between a man and a woman in marriage. The three major sections consist of courtship (1:2–3:5), a wedding (3:6–5:1), and the maturation of marriage (5:2–8:4). Song of Songs describes the beginning of the couple's love, its traits, and power. Although the book contains beautiful poetry, it's a challenging book to understand. Therefore, consider reading it with a commentary such as *The Bible Knowledge Commentary* by John F. Walvoord and Roy B. Zuck.

The Importance of Restraint

Although in this biblical courtship, expressions of sexual desire abound; the lovers also express great sexual restraint. They used restraint because of their deep love and commitment to each other, but they longed for their wedding day. However, after the wedding (3:6-11), an absence of sexual restraint is obvious. Lack of self-control is a sign of weakness and lack of foresight. Please reflect on some Scripture verses.

> *"Do not lust in your heart after her beauty or let her captivate you with her eyes, for the prostitute reduces you to a loaf of bread, and the adulteress preys upon your very life. So is he who sleeps with another man's wife* [even someone's future spouse]; *no one who touches her will go unpunished"* (Proverbs 6:25-26, 29 NIV).

> *"Flee the evil desires of youth, and pursue righteousness, faith, love and peace, along with those who call on the Lord out of a pure heart"* (2 Timothy 2:22 NIV).

The sexual impulse is God-given,
and it must be God-guided.
—James Earl Massey

Do You Value the Dance of the *Initiator and Responder?*

More divine directives from the pen of Solomon express the themes of longing, insecurity, and praise. Solomon, the human writer of the book, Solomon, the pursuer (initiator) provided love, security, and protection to his beloved. The woman (identified as the "beloved") recognized the handsomeness of her lover but valued his pleasant and lovely personality more (1:16-17).

The sense of his protection, the closeness she felt with him, and his attention and expressions of love (2:3-6) were important to her. A woman's sense of security (including financial) and self-worth comes from her husband's protection, intimacy, and attentive love, which will enable her to enjoy a stable marriage.

Displaying spiritual leadership demonstrates protection to a woman. Both true believers, Jill and Tom, dated for months. Although Tom had the potential to be the spiritual leader of a family, currently, he lacked that trait. Hoping Tom would become the spiritual leader wasn't sensible because spiritual leadership should be apparent before marriage. Therefore, Jill stopped dating him.

Since a woman needs to feel loved and treasured, she feels cherished when the man affirms her and gives her affection and attention. Various text phrases show that Solomon loved her beauty, but he was most fascinated with her inner qualities, which he praised. He particularly cherished her responses to his initiations. While a woman responds to love, a man needs respect more than love, and Solomon's beloved respected him.

Contrary to today's thinking in modern culture, God views the male as the initiator (leader) and pursuer, and the woman as the responder. Unfortunately, through films, stories, television, commercials, cartoons, books, or other media, our culture seeks to squash the masculinity of today's men.

Modern dating encourages a reversal of roles of women pursuing men. They pursue by phoning men, writing notes, or dressing indecently (including tight or revealing clothes) to lure men. A woman may phone a man but should avoid a habit of calling. Women should avoid blunt and flirtatious comments or initiating hugs. Today, an aggressive woman might ask a man for a date, and some women even propose marriage. When a woman initiates, she disrespects and nullifies the God-ordained masculinity and leadership of the man. If a woman persists in leading, she will likely carry this behavior into her marriage.

While dating, the man as initiator pursues the woman. He asks her out, he takes the lead on dates, and he is the one who proposes marriage. She responds to his initiations and thus respects his masculinity. Role reversals of the initiator and responder in marriage ignite the battle of the sexes. However, observance of this biblical initiator/responder pattern sets the stage for a healthy marriage.

True Love Comes Slowly in Contrast to Infatuation

Love develops during the dating phase and should continue to grow in marriage. We can't force love; we must wait patiently for it. Anyone who wants a bond similar to Solomon and his beloved must patiently wait for God to develop it in their lives. Like Solomon's beloved, expect problems or conflict during dating. How you resolve them is a part of the process of growing together as a couple considering marriage.

Like couples such as Ruth and Boaz, and Isaac and Rebekah, marriage doesn't require passionate human love at the onset to develop into an enjoyable marriage. However, applications of *agape* love are essential to help a marriage strengthen through adjustments and fine-tuning.

Like flowers that take time to grow and bloom,
let love blossom in its time.

God's Perspective on Sex and Faithfulness

Song of Songs depicts sex in marriage as beautiful, not dirty. The physical magnetism of husband and wife fulfills the longings, and are natural and honorable to God. In addition, Song of Songs honors pleasing qualities in the personalities of the man and the woman. God praises moral purity (4:12), but premarital sex is contrary to God's plans (2:7; 3:5). God expects faithfulness before and after marriage, and He honors that with His blessings (6:3; 7:10; 8:12). Faithfulness in marital love pictures God's love for and commitment to His people and Christ to His bride.

Do You Know When to Seek Guidance?

Though often overlooked, seeking the counsel of your pastor, parents, family members, or believer friends (Proverbs 12:15; 15:22) is an important phase of relationship building. Outside council may have a clearer view of the "big picture" and provide advice to help you avoid future heartaches.

The Lord won't disappoint Christians who seek His guidance. In His sovereignty, our Father knows everything and does all things well. He knew you before you were born. He knew what you would look like, your personality traits, and every detail of your life. Our Father knows your decisions, your career choices, your hopes and dreams, and everything else.

> *God may conceal His purposes*
> *so we will live on His promises.*
>
> —CBZ

He wants you to depend on Him for guidance in all matters including your choice of a marriage partner or your state of singleness. Since God knows whether you will marry and whom you will marry, why worry about it? Didn't God give Eve to Adam? Relax and let the Lord continue to direct your path. *"Trust in the LORD with all your heart, And lean not on your own understanding; In all your ways acknowledge Him, And He shall direct your paths"* (Proverbs 3:5-6). Since the Lord will guide you (if you allow Him to), why be anxious about seeking a mate? He says, *"I will instruct you and teach you in the way you should go; I will guide you with My eye"* (Psalm 32:8).

> *Doing the will of God leaves me no time*
> *for disputing about His plans.*
> —CBZ

Study Questions

Cite Bible verses when you can.

1. What are some unrealistic marriage expectations?

2. Before considering marriage, you must be _____ to making it work.

3. Regarding the maturity sections, which are still underdeveloped in your life?

4. Maturity should come before taking on adult _____ _____.

5. An emotionally mature person takes _____ of his own life, has mental picture of _____, has _____ to fulfill dreams and goals, and has _____ for others.

6. True love with commitment to God's standards will help a couple practice _____ restraint.

7. What three traits does a woman need from her husband to feel secure and valued?

8. What does a man's spiritual leadership offer to a woman?

9. Explain the importance of a man being the initiator and a woman the responder.

10. Faithfulness in marital _____ pictures God's love and _____ to His people, and Christ to His _____.

11. Why is seeking counsel important when you are dating?

12. Why is it important to read admirable books or articles about dating and marriage?

13. Will you listen to Bible-based messages about marriage? (See resource list.)

CHAPTER 4

Is There Something Better Than Modern Dating?

Are you interested in learning a better way to date?

In this chapter you will:

- ♥ Examine various types of modern dating and some of its dangers.

- ♥ Discover principled dating—the alternative to modern dating.

Modern dating, a recent invention primarily practiced in North America, is unknown to 99.5 percent of the world's population. Modern dating practices pose dangers.

Selecting a suitable spouse is a precursor to a satisfying, long-term marriage. Therefore, by examining the pitfalls of modern dating, perhaps individuals will avoid those mistakes and heartaches. Although dating began as a method for searching for a spouse, dating now includes several styles as evaluated below.

Can Casual Dating with Its Pitfalls Be Good?

In casual dating, people not ready for or disinterested in marriage date for fun. Casual dating invites indiscriminate dating, and a potential spouse. They drift from one relationship to another, seeking to satisfy their wants. Instead of waiting and relying on the Lord for guidance, these singles enter the casual or aimless dating game.

> *A selfish heart loves for what it can get*
> *—a Christ-like heart loves for what it can give.*
> —CBZ

For many couples in America's modern dating scene, getting to know the other person—their interests and convictions—seems less important than getting one's wants met. Casual dating often includes casual sex. Self-absorption and a lack of respect for the other person describe this reckless casual dating.

> *For many couples dating is self-serving,*
> *focusing on how good the other person makes one feel,*
> *what he does to please me. Much of the focus is on self.*
> *No one is so empty as when he is filled*
> *with thoughts of himself.*
> —CBZ

A lack of in-depth communication causes the bond to remain superficial. When physical attraction and fun become the focus, dating often follows the repeated pattern of emotional and physical involvement and then break-up.

> *Mary: "Well, what happened when you showed*
> *the girls in the office your new engagement ring?*
> *Did they all admire it?"*
> *Sara: "Better than that, four of them recognized it."*
> —*Best Ever Book of Clean Jokes*

Do You Know Why Serial Monogamy in Dating Is Harmful?

Toward the end of the 20th century, another dating style appeared—serial monogamy that describes a series of serious and exclusive relationships. Serial monogamy and casual dating may encompass short- or long-term relationships. Often, these exclusive couples live together and perhaps consider this simulated marriage.

A misfortune of serial monogamy dating includes the string of broken hearts, the disappointments, and emotional scars that may carry into marriage. When expectations fail, and the fun vanishes during dating, couples drift to somebody new. This pattern of connecting and separating transfers into marriage. When there are tough times or "I'm not enjoying this relationship," then divorce talk begins. Today's random casual dating and serial monogamy are practices for divorce.

Unfortunately, some young people begin dating in middle school or high school. They don't realize that it is after age 18 that significant maturity in judgment happens.

> The world delights to push down the dating age. Even some Christian parents think it is cute to talk about dates in the sixth grade. Wait a minute! Stop to think that through. There is a natural sequence to the dating of young people. They begin by informally dating several persons. Then they date one person. Then they make the decision to get married. If you allow your children to start the first part of that script early, they will arrive at the last part when they are still in great need of mature judgment.
> —John E. Ashbrook, *Family Fundamentals*.

*The foolishness of these dating practices
is like an eight-year-old test-driving one car after another.*

What Do You Think about Dating Services?

The Bible neither condemns nor supports courtship or dating. Some believe in the superiority of online dating over established customs for finding a spouse. About one in five new relationships now begin online, but is online matchmaking a feasible way to find a mate?

*A hopeful young lady listed her requirements
with a computer dating service. She wanted someone
who liked people, wasn't too tall, preferred formal attire,
and enjoyed water sports. The computer followed her
wishes exactly; it sent her a penguin.*

Initially, an honest profile can tell you more additional information about a person than a casual meeting. However, looking good in print isn't always reality—there is lying on profiles. So, proceed with caution when dating someone you have never met in person. When you pursue online dating matches, do an online criminal background check. Although dating services promote "supposed" superiority in their matchmaking, they all have drawbacks. Since matchmaking services seek profit, their claims aren't always trustworthy.

What Are Some Weaknesses of Online Dating?

Two major weaknesses of online dating include overdependence on searching profiles and emphasis on "matching formulas." Studies show that some people lack insight into their personality traits, which may attract or repel someone. Because some people lack understanding of themselves, they may have struggles determining compatibility when browsing profiles. Not until they meet face-to-face will they get a true sense of attraction or lack of it. Since every circumstance is unique, what works for one couple may be disastrous for another as indicated in the following two stories.

Jan, a Christian widow, met Dave through an online dating service. Through emails and phone conversations, they became acquainted. After nearly a year of long-distance dating, they were in love and decided to marry. Since she had a job, two kids, and a house in a Midwestern state, they agreed that Dave would relocate. After only a few months of marriage, Jan and Dave realized they had made a mistake. Day-after-day togetherness revealed obstacles, personality quirks, beliefs, incompatibilities, and parenting dissimilarities unknown during their long-distance courtship. As a result, they divorced within the year.

Randy and Carol, who lived hundreds of miles apart, met through an online dating service. Besides emails and phone calls, they commuted to spend essential time together. The couple prayed, asked counsel from others including their parents, and depended on God's guidance, which resulted in a contented marriage.

What Could Be Better Than Online Dating Services?

Before you give in to seeking a mate with online matchmaking, consider the following. In the past, a blind date was an opportunity to meet and date someone with whom you had a mutual connection, such as a friend or coworker. Online dating takes the blind date to the next level, a higher level of uncertainty and insecurity. Besides the fact that it's impossible for you to know the moral history of an online match, you are exposing yourself to spiritual risks. Don't overestimate your ability to discern and resist a sweet-talking admirer. Online dating can produce superficial personalities with overzealous pursuits of your attention. Wouldn't it be better if your marriage was the result of a friendship built by Jesus Christ and involved likeminded fellowship and service towards the Lord? Online dating is the opposite of this.

Keep God in Online Dating

However, as noted before, online dating isn't forbidden by God. As in all dating, following God's will means emphasizing His principles for selecting a spouse. Therefore, when seeking a mate through dating sites, praying for God's direction and guidance is fundamental.

Much of modern dating is worldly. Worldliness means anything that portrays sin as normal and depicts righteousness as strange. *"For the grace of God that brings salvation has appeared to all men. It teaches us to say "No" to ungodliness and worldly passions and to live self-controlled, upright and godly lives in this present age"* (Titus 2:11-12 NIV). Dating is not inherently wrong, but knowing its dangers and pitfalls can be helpful.

The Danger of Conformity in Dating

Often, immature individuals date because their friends are dating. They date because others date or feel they must avoid being different. With modern dating comes crushes, crashes, and breakups that can harm. Consider this tragic example of a dating teen.

In general, Dylan, 17, was accustomed to having his way—he was popular, had superior grades, had a girlfriend, loved to hunt with his father, and enjoyed a loving family. Therefore, he didn't have much practice coping with disappointment (most teens haven't). For two years, Dylan had exclusively dated Christine. In the fall she went to college while he remained a high school senior. In October, Dylan received a letter from Christine suggesting that they date others to make sure that they were right for each other. Dylan became distraught and depressed, and his parents couldn't console him. A day or two after hearing from Christine, Dylan came home from high school on his lunch hour. Unexpectedly, his parents also came home for lunch, and they had a brief visit with their son before going back to work. When the parents returned later that afternoon, his father discovered his only son had committed suicide.

God commands us not to be conformed (squeezed into a mold; to allow self to be changed) to the world's philosophy. Instead, our Father wants us transformed into Christ-likeness through the Spirit's renewing of our mind with the Word of God (spiritual food). *"And do not be conformed to this world, but be transformed by the renewing of your mind, that you may prove what is that good and acceptable and perfect will of God"* (Romans 12:2). Modern dating has great potential for derailing a Christian's life, especially for teens.

Have You Heard of the Alternative to Modern Dating?

In contrast to modern dating—casual, random, serial monogamy or online dating—would you be interested in another way? After looking at the various types of modern dating, we turn our thoughts to *principled* dating.

Principled dating follows biblical standards and keeps those in mind while dating with the intent of *selecting* a Christian spouse. These standards are principles and commands for Christian living, for sharing the gospel, for marriage, for spiritual growth, and all for the honor and glory of Christ.

Some people consider *principled* dating and *purposeful* dating as the same thing. Using the term purposeful has some problems. *Purposeful* dating can be compared with courtship because couples make known their intent for marriage from the start. Right from the start, the couples' mindset is marriage—we will date and then marry. In *purposeful* dating (like courtship), *marriage* becomes the goal. When marriage doesn't happen, there can be heartaches and hurts from inappropriate expectations. Conversely, in *principled* dating (the focus of this book), the objective is seeking a suitable, Christian mate. In *principled* dating, the objective is *selection,* not marriage.

Study Questions

Cite Scripture verses when possible.

1. What are the pitfalls of casual dating?

2. Why is casual dating inappropriate for the believer?

3. What are the dangers or pitfalls of serial monogamy dating?

4. Where is the focus when a person dates casually or serial monogamy?

5. Why should middle school kids and high school teens refrain from dating?

6. When is a wise or better time to begin dating?

7. What are the pros and cons of online dating?

8. What is the goal of principled dating? How is it different from purposeful dating?

9. Why is principled dating a wise choice for the Christian?

CHAPTER 5

Do You Know Important Principles for Spouse Selection?

Are you interested in learning specifics about principled dating?
Do you know the fundamentals of selecting a spouse?
Have you thought about dating conduct and manners?

In this chapter you will:

- ♥ Learn about principled dating.

- ♥ Consider biblical essentials of choosing a spouse.

- ♥ Consider practical dating guidelines.

Three Biblical Points to Remember

Before exploring principled dating, consider biblical points regarding marriage.

- ♥ *Some were arranged.* Genesis 24 provides an example of an arranged marriage in which Abraham sent his servant to seek a wife for Abraham's son, Isaac. God orchestrated the servant's meeting with Rebekah, who became Isaac's wife. God works behind the scenes, even in your life.

- ♥ *Some were practicality.* Romantic love wasn't necessarily involved. Ruth and Boaz had other reasons besides romantic love to draw them together; other circumstances than mutual love brought David and Michal together (1 Samuel 18). Further biblical examples of circumstances other than marrying for love include Jacob and Leah, and Hosea and Gomer.

- ♥ *Parental guidance was involved.* Parents, especially the father, involved themselves. However, parents would often keep their child's wishes in mind. In particular cases, parents would seek to dissuade their adult child. We read in Judges 14 that Samson's parents disapproved of his selection of a wife. We see here that parental involvement is biblical regardless of the age. Since parental guidance is biblical, do not regard it as meddling.

Ideally, Christian couples will follow principles of Scripture to determine whether marriage is God's will for them. You may do something that God may permit, yet not be in His perfect will. Keep in mind the Lord gives His best to those who follow His will! Determining mate selection and whether marriage is God's will for you at this time and with this person is the goal of principled dating.

Fundamental Factors of Principled Dating

Principled dating

- ♥ Is a serious matter in contrast to modern dating.

- ♥ Has the objective of spouse selection.

- ♥ Applies God's principles to dating.

- ♥ Includes prayers for discerning God's choice of a spouse and for discernment in recognizing God's will for your life, which could include singleness.

- ♥ Includes seeking godly counsel (input) from parents (if possible), your pastor, and friends who are walking with the Lord.

Necessary Christian Life Principles for Selecting a Spouse

Avoid seeking the will of God through subjective and often incorrect feelings. Feelings should be the trailer, not the driver of our lives. Instead, be aligned with principles of Scripture. Practicing fundamental biblical principles precludes choosing a mate. First, each person must decide personally about the following in this order.

1. Who will be my Messiah (Savior)?

2. Who will be my Master?

3. What is my Mission in life?

4. Who will be my Mate?

After settling these issues personally, then evaluate a possible mate with the following:

- √ *Destiny.* Is this person saved? Is the person a genuine believer in Christ, since God commands us to marry a believer (2 Corinthians 6:14)?

- √ *Doctrine.* Is this person doctrinally sound? How can we make decisions together if we don't have the same biblical standards (Amos 3:3)?

- √ *Desire.* Does this person want to follow the will of God?

√ *Direction.* What is the general direction of this person's life? What is their relationship with Christ? Is Christ his or her priority?

God will lead you to His true and perfect will as you look to Him. *"But seek first the kingdom of God and His righteousness, and all these things shall be added to you"* (Matthew 6:33). As Warren Wiersbe affirms, "When the Word of God is in our hearts, then the will of God is in our hearts, and we obey Him wholeheartedly."

Keep a Mindset of Biblical Principles When Dating for Spouse Selection

Just as marriage takes nurturing work and success isn't automatic, a wise believer will follow God's principles during the process of spouse selection. The previous chapters presented biblical principles to keep in mind for living, and for selective dating.

In review, the basics are listed below.

- ♥ Make Christ the center of your life so He will take the spotlight in your dating.

- ♥ Understand God's purpose for marriage.

- ♥ Understand the principles of *agape* love, respect, and service in a marriage.

Living your faith by displaying agape love
towards your dating partner establishes
positive practices for marriage.

Eight Practical Suggestions for Single Women

1. Seek the Lord's will in every circumstance.

2. When someone of interest asks you out for dinner, you could say "yes" without having to *love* him. Dinner or lunch provides an opportunity in a public place for becoming acquainted.

3. A man's invitation is just that, an invitation, not a proposal.

4. Be yourself and be friendly.

5. Sometimes poor first impressions are accurate. However, sometimes despite first impressions, some men are hidden gems. Give him a chance to win your attention. Prayer and discernment are relevant.

6. If you aren't interested in him, kindly tell him. Understand how to give a firm "no" without embarrassing him. Gently refusing him includes thanking him. Make sure your body language and your tone of voice display consideration.

    Examples:

    Since Becky didn't want to date Paul, she honestly told him with a kind tone how she felt. She knew it could hurt to lead him on or date him out of pity. Becky didn't lie.

    Mary simply said politely, "No, thank you." No explanations are necessary, but if you have a good reason, you could share it. Mary understood that keeping her response short and direct was best. She was careful not to put him down or make herself appear superior, just explained her perspective.

Donna felt flattered when Dave invited her on a date. She didn't want to date him. She knew she must politely refuse, thus treating Dave as she would want to be treated, better yet as Jesus treats us. She knew that it takes courage for a man to ask a woman for a date, so with a calm and gentle spirit, she declined the invitation. She tactfully avoided listing reasons about why he doesn't match what she is seeking in a man.

Lisa knew if she offered, "let's just be friends," she might falsely encourage him. If she said, "I'm busy next week," or "I'm not ready to date right now," could give false hope.

Instead of honesty, some people try to please, which accomplishes nothing. We shouldn't say "yes" to avoid hurting feelings or over-apologize for how we feel. Just a firm "no" can suffice. If he doesn't accept your answer, repeat it.

*An obnoxious guy would not accept
"No, thank you" from a woman he wanted to date.
Finally, she gave him the number for the county zoo;
she never saw him again.*

Call your dad into the situation if the man won't take the hint that you aren't interested. This recommendation mainly applies to daughters still living at home, since fathers are the protector of the family, particularly of their daughters.

7. Let the man pay for the dinner.

8. End a dating experience by meeting face-to-face. Voice your concerns about your differences or things that concern you as

you date; then your desire to break up will not be a *surprise*. Be clear and concise, using kindness and consideration.

Seven Practical Tips for Single Men

1. Seek the Lord's will in all circumstances.

2. Ask a woman for a date. Most women would like to go out and will say "yes," but you need to ask.

3. Realize that asking a woman out to dinner isn't the same as a marriage proposal. If she is living at home, she may respond that she needs to ask her father first; take that seriously and respect the decision. Always respect the concerns of the young woman's parents. Remember—parental involvement is biblical and not meddling.

4. If a circumstance causes you hurt or disturbs you, you need to talk to God about that and seek godly counsel. Ask God to heal your feelings and give you the courage to date again.

5. Pay for dinner.

6. Work for a living. Women usually don't want to date a man who doesn't work. Of course, temporary unemployment isn't the same as disinterest or unwillingness to work.

*In seeking a model husband,
choosing a working model is sensible.*

7. When you feel the need to end your dating experience, there are several points to keep in mind. How men break up says a lot about their character.

Guidelines include but are not limited to the following:

- √ Don't break up without warning. Instead, as you date share things you disagree with and what makes you uncomfortable.

- √ Face-to-face discussion is respectful and takes more courage. Give your undivided attention (no texting, phone calls, or email checking) during this meeting.

- √ Be clear and provide some concrete reasons why you want to end the association. Don't criticize or belittle your date. You don't need a record of wrongs, but have some real reasons that led you to this decision, why you don't think you are right for each other. Don't be vague, which may give hope for the future. There should be no confusion that it's over.

Timely Dating Advice for Men and Women

1. Stay close to God through Bible reading, hearing His word, and prayer.

2. Pray that God would prepare you and make you a suitable mate.

   Don't hunt for the right person;
   instead, ask if I am the right person in Christ?

3. Trust God with your life and your dating time.

4. Pray for each date. Pray that your words and behavior honor your Savior. Pray for your dating partner.

5. Seek out public places where you can have private conversations.

6. Have fun. Be yourself.

7. In general, don't marry because of physical attraction before you have gotten to know the person. Just because you are lonely, don't marry someone who shows an interest in you. Never ignore warning signs!

8. Communicate, Communicate, and Communicate! Unfortunately, texting has decreased face-to-face communication. Because texting is impersonal, avoid it. Use texting for essentials such as confirming or canceling a date.

   When is texting not helpful in your contacts? While texting can be a helpful tool, some misuse it to gossip about another, even someone in the same room. Unfortunately, people use texting for every micro movement in their lives. Texting instead of socializing with others in social gatherings is simply rude. Some individuals use texting and emailing as escape routes. People can ignore messages, avoid answering questions, and fail to notice hurt feelings in the other person.

   During person-to-person communication, the tone of voice (nuances) and the implications are obvious, as are facial expressions, but not in texting. So misinterpretations when texting can cause anger. No one can show genuine care and consideration through inanimate words and symbols.

   For a good impression, ask for a date in person or via the phone. You may not get a reply to a text message if she is busy with something. Texting may suggest a lack of self-confidence, portray laziness, or give some other negative impression.

Dating via texting or face-to-face isn't the same. Find enjoyment in getting to know each other by communicating in person. Adults who model maturity and proper etiquette talk in person.

9. Waiting for God's plan for your life is the best plan.

> *"Many are the plans in a man's heart, but it is the LORD's purpose that prevails"* (Proverbs 19:21 NIV).

Study Questions

Provide Scripture verses when possible.

1. What is principled dating?

2. Name the four basic spiritual principles (all start with "M") for selecting a suitable mate.

3. List the four secondary principles (all start with "D") for evaluating a prospective mate.

4. What did you find most helpful in this chapter?

CHAPTER 6

How to Avoid Infatuation Mistakes

Do you know the distinctions between infatuation and love?
What is dating idolatry?
What is *agape* love and why is it important?

In this chapter we will:

- ♥ Discover the harm associated with infatuation.

- ♥ Examine dating idolatry and its link with infatuation.

- ♥ Learn truths about genuine love.

In the modern dating pattern, feelings drive individuals. Dating creates a bond, especially for women, and both men and women can mistake the feelings of infatuation for love. When feelings lead, individuals do what is right in their own eyes, and often the sexual bond develops.

What Is Infatuation?

Typically experienced by adolescents, but also seen in adults, infatuation is a strong emotion, a temporary romantic attachment. Based on emotion, infatuation frequently occurs at the onset when the attraction is most intense. Other infatuation symptoms include urgency, panic, jealousy, intensity, sexual desire, apprehension, high-risk choices, and irresponsible disregard of values. Consumed by emotion, an infatuated person has irrational cravings towards someone. Infatuation can be "lust"—a strong desire or yearning.

In contrast with self-centered and temporary infatuation, human or natural love suggests an emotion of intense affection for another person, an emotion between two people. Qualities of human love consist of trustworthiness, confidence, a willingness to sacrifice and to compromise. Let's compare infatuation with love.

What Are the Distinctions Between Infatuation and Love?

Adapted from a message by Kurt Witzig, at Duluth Bible Church, Duluth, MN, and the following online resources:

www.eharmony.com/blog/the-difference-between-lust-love-and-infatuation/

Infatuation is self-centered, occupied with one's own needs and comforts.

♥ **Love concerns itself with the needs of others. Jesus Christ modeled *agape* love by serving others and giving His life for others.**

Infatuation happens suddenly, and people describe it as *love at first sight.* Since it happens quickly and is superficial, it can burn off rapidly.

♥ **Love grows gradually as you get to know the other person.**

Infatuation suggests a reckless commitment to fulfilling one's all-consuming lust.

Infatuation, an intense euphoria, risks everything for the next rush of adrenaline.

♥ Love genuinely commits and has genuine intentions.

♥ Love considers another's feelings before acting.

♥ Love has effective communication and suitable expectations.

Infatuation brings emptiness—a result of choices made during temporary lust.

♥ Love understands that knowing someone is necessary for raising a family.

♥ Love is enduring, founded on security, peace, and a solid partnership.

Infatuation expects to find happiness in another.

♥ Love expects to achieve happiness and looks first to Christ for joy.

♥ Love exhibits deep affection, contentment, and confidence.

Infatuation is dependent (needy) and relies on a pseudo feeling of love and physical attraction. Fascination love obsesses on closeness with someone at any cost, including compromising values.

♥ Love is an interdependent partnership encouraged by the individuality of the person loved.

Infatuation is fragile, unpredictable, and unable to think rationally.

♥ Love is a pattern for living and deepens with time.

Infatuation is irrational and incapable of discerning what is true and valuable.

♥ Love is guided by standards, can discern, and has stability.

Infatuation has a false commitment, if any, and is temporary and self-serving. Fake love may produce closeness, but frequently the feeling is one-sided.

♥ Love comprises commitment based on genuine actions of doing what is best for another and includes serving another. Love is selfless and other-focused.

Infatuation includes assorted feelings usually caused by physical attraction.

Infatuation believes similar feelings and thinking is synonymous with being in love.

♥ Love seeks to know the other person's traits, interests, goals, and values that create close mutual bonds; it concentrates on internals.

Infatuation ignores others and abandons family and friends.

♥ Love enjoys social contacts with others and cultivates friendships.

Infatuation is demanding or possessive. Fascination love is about what "I want or need."

♥ Love permits freedom to the other person; it accepts the person as is.

Infatuation needs favorable conditions to survive.

♥ Love develops and can grow under adverse circumstances.

Infatuation idealizes the feeling beyond reality.

♥ Love takes comfort in realism.

Infatuation leads to frustration.

♥ Love advances to satisfaction.

Infatuation excludes God in life planning.

♥ Love includes God in the planning and depends on the Lord.

Eight Ways to Tell If You're in Love
True love distinguishes between a person and a body.
True love always generates respect.
True love is self-giving.
True love can thrive without physical expression.
True love seeks to build a relationship.
True love embraces responsibility.
True love can postpone gratification.
True love is commitment.

—Erwin Lutzer

Infatuation Can Lead to Dating Idolatry

Fascinated with another, an infatuated person imagines the way he or she wants a relationship. Fascinations can cause another dating danger—idolatry. Couples unknowingly yield to idolatry when they fixate on each other to the exclusion of others. Obsessed Christians may also exclude their Savior. What you think about most becomes your god. When individuals turn away from God, turn their thoughts and attention to another person, and lose himself or herself in that other person, they practice idolatry.

Song lyrics portray idolatry. For example,

- ♥ "You're my soul and my heart's inspiration."

- ♥ "Only you can make a change in me; you are my destiny."

- ♥ "I can't go through one night without you . . . I can't live without you."

Some couples can easily become involved in idolatry, as stated in these song lyrics. Their mindset is "Turn your eyes upon Joey (or Crystal), and the things of this world will grow strangely dim" versus the true words of this hymn: "Turn your eyes upon Jesus . . ." Often, individuals stop living for Christ. He isn't their priority. Modern dating encourages self-absorbed people who desire what they can *get* from their dating partner.

> *When you are wrapped up in yourself,*
> *you are overdressed.*
> —CBZ

Dating individuals can become distracted and slip into idolatry because their emotions mesmerize them. Regardless of age, feelings of fake love can trick us. Feelings of infatuation (fake love) may cause symptoms such as this short list.

- ♥ How *love* makes you *feel*

- ♥ You lose your appetite or have trouble sleeping

- ♥ You are apprehensive

- ♥ You have feelings of jealousy

- ♥ You are obsessed, thinking of the one you love

Instead of preoccupation with another, consider the following questions. Who loves you the most (Romans 5:8)? Who alone completes you (Colossians 2:10)? Who understands you best (Hebrews 4:15-16)? Who is always with you and who is most loyal (Hebrews 13:5-6)? Believing these truths about your Savior will enable you to profess boldly, "The Lord is my helper, I will not fear; the Lord satisfies me with good things."

We have a Savior who satisfies us, who desires the abundant life for us (John 10:10). Instead of living for another, God commands us to live for Christ (Galatians 2:19 NIV). *"You shall love the LORD your God with all your heart, with all your soul, and with all your strength"* (Deuteronomy 6:5). When we fail to make God the priority, we fill up our souls with people or things of this world, but we never feel complete. However, an intimate relationship with Christ offers a fulfilled life—the abundant life—unlike anything else.

> *When the Lord Jesus Christ is enjoyed,*
> *things unlike Him drop off like fading leaves.*
> —Miles Stanford

What Do You Think about Love at First Sight?

Worldly love—infatuation—is Satan's deception, which clouds our thinking. Young women especially believe in the love at first sight deception. Definitions of romance include an ardent emotional attachment or involvement between people; a strong, sometimes short-lived attachment or fascination. Today's present view of love perpetrates romance in books, soap operas, and movies—portraying love as just happening. Your feelings of excitement may deceive you into thinking it's love when it's merely infatuation. Not every relationship starts with infatuation. Be discerning, some couples may meet and marry quickly and it may true love.

By nature, people deceive and are deceived. *"The heart is deceitful above all things, And desperately wicked; Who can know it?"* (Jeremiah 17:9). While dating, individuals—especially young women—fall for lies and believe the deceit of flattery. Ungodly men are self-seeking, saying whatever it takes to gratify their selfish craving. *"For those who are such do not serve our Lord Jesus Christ, but their own belly, and by smooth words and flattering speech deceive the hearts of the simple"* (Romans 16:18). Additional verses include *"Save me, O LORD, from lying lips and from deceitful tongues"* (Psalm 120:2 NIV). *"Take heed that no one deceives you"* (Matthew 24:4). *"Keep your tongue from evil and your lips from speaking lies"* (Psalm 34:13 NIV). The deceits and lies regarding love in the dating culture is a real danger.

Flattery is manipulation, not communication.

Have You Heard about the Hormones of Infatuation?

You have probably heard people comment, "It's just hormones," and then chuckle as they refer to infatuation. Now here is the rest of the story. Research shows that hormones do produce infatuation. The hormones give individuals a warm feeling, dreaminess, lack of appetite, butterflies in the stomach, and other symptoms of physical attraction.

One *love* hormone called phenylethylamine (PEA) along with several other hormones and neurotransmitters are involved with the occurrence of love. PEA levels also can increase with high-intensity activities like jogging and by consuming large amounts of chocolate or specific drugs. When someone experiences infatuation or *love,* brain levels of dopamine and norepinephrine increase, as does testosterone (since lust is involved). Another hormone, oxytocin, plays a role in "love" since physical touching increases this hormone. PEA, along with the other hormones and neurotransmitters, produce a "high" feeling.

Sources:

PEA–*The Hormone of Love* by Dario Nardi, Ph.D. visited April 2, 2017, http://www.biotype.net/types/article3_2005.htm

The Plunge of Pleasure by Deborah Blum, published on September 1, 1997, https://www.psychologytoday.com/articles/199709/the-plunge-pleasure

Infatuation and Marriage Do Not Mix Well

When an individual mistakes infatuation for love, significant problems result. When someone transitions out of infatuation, hormone levels drop. In this phase, people can continue into a stronger bond or break up. An infatuated couple many become bored, and they may separate. If couples marry while under the power of infatuation, they may divorce when the *high* of infatuation disappears. Couples may say they don't love each other anymore or fell out of love, so they begin a cycle of changing marriages in search of the infatuation *highs*.

Lust, a response to appearance, may quickly fade since it emphasizes immediate satisfaction. That's why an object—a car you wanted or a relationship—may in time fail to hold your interest. The newness wears off and you seek some new high. The lust of the flesh is never satisfied. *"So I say, live by the Spirit, and you will not gratify the desires of the sinful nature.* (Galatians 5:16 NIV).

"What is it to 'walk in the Spirit'" (Galatians 5:16)?

To walk in the Spirit is not self-occupation, nor even occupation with the Spirit. Walking according to the Spirit is occupation with the Lord Jesus. When the believer looks to the Lord Jesus, depends upon Him, draws all he needs from Him— if the Lord Jesus is his all, then the believer walks in the Spirit.

—A. C. Gaebelein, quoted in Miles Stanford, *None But The Hungry Heart, 8-6.*

What Does Scripture Tell Us Regarding Feelings?

God's Word tells us that our heart—the inner person including the mind and will— holds our feelings. God commands us to guard our hearts (Proverbs 4:23). We should guard our hearts so emotions won't control us, to avoid lust, and escape the thinking of worldly love. We guard our hearts when we give our whole heart, will, and mind to God's Word. The Spirit through the Word will mold and shape your thinking into conformity with the mind of Christ (Philippians 2:5), including His *agape* love mindset in you.

Don't let your feelings direct your life. Infatuation isn't necessarily a sin in itself, but it matters how we handle it or if we let it control us. Dwelling on desires can lead you to sin. David allowed his lustful feeling to dictate his behavior, which resulted in sin with Bathsheba (2 Samuel 11). Samson let his feelings direct him when he saw a young Philistine woman (Judges 14:1). Although emotions are God-given, they must not guide us. The heart isn't a trustworthy source of feelings (Jeremiah 17:9).

Why are emotions untrustworthy? Feelings are unreliable when they are products of our flesh—the old sin nature (like a Satan nature). The carnal mind follows the sin nature, which opposes God and is unyielding to God's will. Feelings themselves aren't inherently good or bad. The problem is they sometimes guide us to things that give us good feelings, regardless if it is God's will or not.

Did you know "follow your heart"—your emotions
—is NOT biblical advice?

What Are the Consequences of Allowing Feelings to Lead?
1. Believers led by feelings are frequently carnal—out of fellowship with God.

2. People guided by feelings have unpredictable moods. Since feelings are unstable, they can be like a roller coaster.

3. Individuals led by emotions may display irrationality, stubbornness, and self-absorption.

4. Individuals ruled by feelings usually reject counsel and wisdom.

5. Emotion-led people impulsively base decisions on feelings, not facts.

6. Those led by emotion are usually miserable.

7. People ruled by feelings frequently exhibit unreliability.

8. Believers who walk by feelings instead of faith may become unusable for God's plan.

Let the Spirit Guide You, Not Your Feelings.

Listen to the Word of God and let it direct your thinking and conduct (Proverbs 3:5-6). *"Your word I have hidden in my heart, That I might not sin against You!"* (Psalm 119:11). Believe the truths of God's Word, and you will be less likely to yield to the world's lies.

Set the boundaries of moral purity ahead of time and understand the power of temptation. Individuals often underestimate the power of temptation but overestimate their capacity to defeat sin themselves. God warns us, *"Watch and pray so that you will not fall into temptation. The spirit is willing, but the body is weak"* (Matthew 26:41 NIV). Realize that when temptation comes, they fail because they have spent time focusing on the world's lies. When they aren't grounded in God's principles, they are vulnerable to fickle feelings and sin.

Trusting God's promises is the best weapon against temptation and deceptions. Living by faith is the key to the Christian life, *"for we walk by, not by sight"* (2 Corinthians 5:7). Faith in God's standards is truer than anything you feel or experience. *"The grass withers, the flower fades, But the word of our God stands forever"* (Isaiah 40:8). God will never lead you contrary to His Word irrespective of the force of your feelings.

The Word of God anchors and stabilizes our feelings.

Let your emotions emerge from biblical truth. For example, don't look for love in the wrong places; instead, look to the promises of the Word of God. *"Yes, I have loved you with an everlasting love; Therefore with lovingkindness I have drawn you"* (Jeremiah 31:3). *"I have been crucified with Christ and I no longer live, but Christ lives in me. The life I live in the body, I live by faith in the Son of God, who loved me and gave himself for me"* (Galatians 2:20 NIV).

God's *Agape* Love Preserves and Strengthens Human Love

In this chapter, we examined infatuation—*fake love.* Now let's conclude with *agape* love. Insightful believers will see the value of *agape* love and avoid infatuation's control. *"He who trusts in his own heart is a fool, But whoever walks wisely will be delivered"* (Proverbs 28:26). Our thinking must control our feelings. Therefore, by rejecting current thinking about love, we won't be fooled.

In conclusion, the Bible speaks of a God-given natural love between a man and a woman, which God's *agape* love preserves and strengthens. Why? *Agape* love is action-based, not feeling-based so this love *does* what is best for another in light of eternity despite the personal cost. The wavering, emotion-based love of infatuation pales in comparison with the strong, *agape* love of Christ, which His Spirit produces through us by faith. We close by reflecting on God's specific *agape* love verses.

> *"Love is patient, love is kind. It does not envy, it does not boast, it is not proud.*
>
> *⁵ It is not rude, it is not self-seeking, it is not easily angered, it keeps no record of wrongs.*
>
> *⁶ Love does not delight in evil but rejoices with the truth.*

⁷ It always protects, always trusts, always hopes, always perseveres.

⁸ Love never fails" (1 Corinthians 13:4-8 (NIV).

Study Questions

Use Scripture verses whenever possible.

1. What are some characteristics of infatuation?

2. What are the dangers of allowing infatuation—fake love to control you?

3. What are some traits of human love?

4. In contrast to infatuation and human love, what is the definition of *agape* love?

5. What have you learned from this chapter?

CHAPTER 7

What Is a Proper Friendship?

How would you keep friendship from crossing the intimacy line?
Have you considered the dangers of premature intimacy?
What is defrauding a future mate?

This chapter will:

- ♥ Examine several types of intimacy.

- ♥ Help you determine when a relationship should end or continue.

- ♥ Caution you about defrauding a future spouse.

How Friendships Help Prepare You for Marriage

God's Word instructs us to choose our friends wisely (Proverbs 12:26a). How much more carefully ought we choose a spouse for life? Don't be afraid to talk with members of the opposite sex. Dismiss the assumption that singles only talk to those of the opposite sex whom they are interested in marrying. Instead, interacting and developing many friendships with the opposite sex will help you better understand the opposite sex. Building Christian friendships with the opposite sex will help you select your future spouse. Attraction to someone may be the spark that leads to a friendship and then to love.

What Is Intimacy?

In contrast to the modern sexual implications, intimacy is a broad term. In sharing one's life, intimacy refers to close familiarity, the closeness between people including the intimacy between a husband and wife. Other synonyms for intimacy include togetherness, deep friendship, affection, or warmth. Intimacy means total sharing of one's life. Companionship is the heart of a close relationship.

In His wisdom, God has given human beings
the capacity for companionship.

Intimacy is sharing your life with another that involves getting to know another without trying to change him or her. Intimacy includes an exchange of giving and receiving between two people, such as a hug that illustrates two-way intimacy of both giving and receiving.

Physical intimacy refers to sharing the *body* in a nurturing, platonic manner. If you ask, "May I give you a hug?" you offer to nurture someone. When you ask, "May I have a hug?" you seek closeness.

Emotional intimacy includes sharing *feelings*. Couples express their joys, fears, frustrations, sorrows, and even anger with each other. Expressing or verbalizing anger is the opposite of yelling and screaming at the other person or even hitting. *"But if you bite and devour one another, beware lest you be consumed by one another!"* (Galatians 5:15). Emotional intimacy means that you share distressing feelings and pleasant ones. Finding respectful ways to share disagreeable feelings is challenging but not impossible.

Intellectual intimacy refers to sharing your thoughts and opinions, such as discussing a book, movie, or play. Closeness can come from knowing that you share similar opinions on social, political, or other issues. Attending an event together may increase your intellectual closeness. Sharing biblical truths can provide intellectual intimacy. You don't need to have the same education, but a need for knowledge together feeds your common spirit. Intellectual closeness develops when you share your thoughts.

Deep intimacy can also come without words. A knowing glance (or a wink) that you give each other because you understand something you see or hear illustrates deep intimacy.

Social intimacy occurs when spending time together. Going to an athletic event, a concert, bowling, playing a board game, or taking a walk together illustrate social intimacy. Life centers on activity that promotes a sense of closeness, even if it's just talking.

Sexual intimacy consists of sharing the *body* in a sexual manner, which God designed for marriage only. The Lord planned this total self-giving as a celebration of the love between a married man and woman. *"Therefore a man shall leave his father and mother and be joined to his wife, and they shall become one flesh"* (Genesis 2:24).

Spiritual intimacy, the highest form of intimacy, is often the most neglected. Our attachment to Christ should be obvious during dating and included in the spiritual bonding with each other. Sharing God's Word with each other and praying together bring closeness and encourages trust. When you let your date hear your heartfelt prayers of petition or thanks, he or she comes to know you better. Once you know your date well and trust him or her not to hurt you in any way, you are prone to honesty and vulnerability and risk the unknown.

With knowledge of another comes hurt and dissatisfaction. Since we are sinful human beings, we will fail and disappoint each other. We might say something negative or judgmental, or we might display thoughtless or self-centered behaviors. When trust is broken, or feelings are hurt, we can take them to the Lord in prayer. The actions of *agape* love will make changes where necessary, apologize, and will forgive. Such behaviors demonstrate active intimacy in the spiritual realm.

What Are the Boundaries Between Friendship and Intimacy?

The word "intimacy" has taken on sexual implications, including romantic or passionate involvement, and the term "intimate relationship" often implies sexual activity. Regrettably, many people consider sexual activity normal and acceptable while dating. As Christians, we should adhere to God's standard of sexual intimacy that God restricts to a man and a woman within the confines of marriage.

For an enduring marriage, friendship should come before intimacy.

How Can Friendships Cross the Line?

Male-Female Friendships can create real dangers in the world's dating process. Friendships can easily lead to intimacy because some romance is always involved.

Male-Female Friendships are romantically stimulating. Events such as biking, going to the mall, hanging out, or just talking and spending time together alone spark a romantic charge. Spending time together can easily lead from friendship to an intimacy reserved for a future spouse.

Male-Female Friendships should be good-natured, reserving personal disclosures for principled dating. Socializing should include group settings with other friends, family gatherings, or mission work. Some forms of intimacy are for married couples only. Therefore, male-female friendships must keep the boundaries between friendship and intimacy. Friendships don't need to stop unless they begin to drift towards intimacy. So when you marry your spouse, that *other* friendship won't negatively affect your marriage.

How do friendship and intimacy fit in a relationship? Though not essential, becoming acquainted through friendship paves the way for principled dating. If possible, get to know a possible marriage partner in public settings like group activities, church events, evangelism outreach, or at work. Join community clubs or activities (photography club, volleyball, or a civic band), do volunteer work, or spend time with family and with friends. As two people get to know each other's interests and convictions, they may become attracted to each other and develop a friendship.

Friendship may lead to a soaring romance or it may not. The friendship may begin to deepen towards emotional or intellectual intimacy. Before friendship crosses the line into intimacy, individuals must prayerfully evaluate whether they want to proceed into principled dating. Friendship may reach the border of intimacy, but emotional intimacy doesn't belong in a male-female *friendship* not pursuing marriage. If either person doesn't want marriage, then stop seeing each other to prevent defrauding.

Friends don't always become good marriage prospects.

How Can You Defraud a Future Spouse?

In addition to stealing somebody's money or private property, defrauding can mean to "deprive of a right." When a couple crosses the line between friendship and intimacy, they may defraud a future spouse.

A person can defraud another by dominating time, which may lead to assorted intimacies between parties uninterested in marrying each other. Individuals may spend too much time together as friends or share personal information. When you spend excessive time with someone you also monopolizes their time, and as a result, cheat (defraud) someone else of that specific time.

When single individuals participate in immorality, they defraud their future spouses. They defraud two future spouses of the right to exclusive sexual intimacy. Virginity is the heritage you contribute to your marriage. Recall the Scriptures regarding defrauding another. *"For this is the will of God, your sanctification: that you should abstain from sexual immorality; that each of you should know how to possess his own vessel in sanctification and honor, not in passion of lust, like the Gentiles who do not know God; that no one should take advantage of and defraud his brother in this matter, because the Lord is the avenger of all such, as we also forewarned you and testified"* (1 Thessalonians 4:3-6).

Defrauding takes place in the emotional sphere. By developing an emotional bond apart from principled dating, you are defrauding a future mate. Elizabeth Elliot cautions, "Never say to a woman that you 'love her' unless you plan to marry her or you can damage her emotionally." Friends must guard against engaging in various intimacies reserved for someone's future spouse.

How can demonstrating agape love protect against defrauding? Agape love doesn't monopolize the time of another or cross lines of intimacy with a friend. When friendship borders on intimacy, *agape* love seeks to protect another from emotional hurts. Be alert to notice when your friendship hugs the line of closeness, pray for God's guidance and direction. Both you and your friend should discuss your present status and honestly determine your intentions. That is, do both of you desire to proceed to *principled* dating to determine whether each one would be an appropriate spouse for the other. If not, you need to stop seeing each other to avoid possible defrauding.

> *Avoid defrauding anyone's future spouse.*
> *Until you marry someone, he or she*
> *may be a future spouse, or even your own.*

Why You Should Avoid Intimacy without Commitment

Two emotions that occur with premature intimacies of dating are *jealousy or possessiveness* in which a person considers that "you belong to him." In reality: Where is the ring? Where's the commitment? Where's the promise? In opposition to a possessive person's thinking, only a marriage commitment is binding.

> We build a solid foundation for love by moving toward commitment at the same rate we move toward physical intimacy. All along the way the privileges of growing intimacy carry with them the responsibilities of growing commitment so that the ultimate intimacy in sexual intercourse coincides with the ultimate commitment in the covenant of marriage.
>
> —Richard Foster

Intimacy must come with commitment. Unfortunately, temporary intimacy often happens in today's superficial, modern dating. A selfish individual with little understanding of intimacy often selects an unsuitable marriage partner.

Intimacy without commitment risks a healthy, long-lasting marriage.

> People being what they are, it is no great achievement to woo some unstable person into a short-lived intimacy. It takes a great deal more character and finesse to make a long-term marriage into a romantic, blooming love affair. And the depth of affection and the freedom of total emotional expression that marriage provides is something experimenters can never know.
>
> —M.P. Horban

Study Questions

Provide Scripture verses or principles when possible.

1. In it's broadest term, intimacy refers to sharing one's _____.

2. At the heart of intimacy is _____.

3. List the ways you could defraud a future spouse.

4. How does *agape* love protect another from being defrauded?

5. Explain how intimacy without commitment risks a healthy, long-lasting marriage.

6. What will you apply from this chapter?

CHAPTER 8

Do You Have Dating Discernment?

What's the harm in dating an unsaved person?
What do you need to know about dating a carnal believer?
Can you recognize abuse in a dating experience?

In this chapter you will:

- ♥ Learn more about dating discernment.

- ♥ Examine the spiritual warnings and dangers of dating an unsaved person.

- ♥ Become aware of some risks with dating a carnal believer.

- ♥ Discover how to identify some warning signs of dating abuse.

What's Wrong with Dating an Unbeliever?

Individuals often disagree with others about dating an unbeliever, arguing that they are "just dating; we aren't going to get married." Although dating doesn't always lead to marriage, people deceive themselves believing this practice is harmless. A Christian dating an unsaved person runs the risk of drifting from obedience and dependence on the Lord Jesus. *"Can two walk together unless they are agreed?"* (Amos 3:3). The unsaved may hinder the Spirit-filled life of the believer.

Because God commands a believer and an unsaved person must not marry, a believer should not date an unbeliever. *"Do not be bound together with unbelievers; for what partnership have righteousness and lawlessness, or what fellowship has light with darkness?"* (2 Corinthians 6:14 NASB). Since a believer and an unsaved person don't have Christ in common, they have no spiritual fellowship. Christians shouldn't even think they can date unbelievers, hoping to lead them to Christ, because the unsaved may not be interested. Instead, pray for their receptivity to the gospel.

> *An unequally yoked dating couple travels two different paths that hinder a Christ-focused unifying bond of spiritual intimacy.*

What's wrong with missionary dating? Though more prevalent in youth, missionary dating can deceive anyone. Unsaved men may be willing to discuss the gospel, but often they are only interested in the woman. Their eagerness to discuss salvation may only suggest their level of attraction. Even if the person just accepted Christ, avoid distractions for spiritual growth by withdrawing from the person.

A spiritually growing young woman was dating a Christian man who wasn't interested in spiritual matters. She asked him if he would like to attend Bible study or church with her. Although he didn't seem interested, he accompanied her because she asked. In time, she realized that she had unwittingly taken his role as spiritual leader. Because she wanted her future husband to be the spiritual leader, she stopped seeing him.

Marrying an unbeliever sometimes works out, but those unequally yoked suffer consequences. The unsaved person has no joy or peace in the Lord, which can discourage the believer spouse. Also, when you decide contrary to God's will, you lose blessings God planned for you.

How to Determine If Someone Is Saved

Perhaps you don't know how to discover whether your date or the person you may consider dating is a believer. The next example illustrates the wrong way to question someone about salvation. Since Ted wanted to date a believer in Jesus Christ, he questioned Anne about her eternal destiny. He asked "yes" or "no" leading questions such as "Do you believe in Jesus Christ as your Savior?" "Do you believe in faith alone in Jesus Christ alone by grace alone?" Anne responded "yes" to each question, so Ted believed Anne was a believer. He continued to date her and eventually married her.

Ted's Christian friends doubted her salvation and in time discovered that she was a non-practicing religious person. Anne believed in Christ but also believed she must do good deeds and display good behavior to enter heaven. To add anything suggests that Christ's work was not enough—"I must add something." If Ted had known how to question specifically and avoided leading questions or simple "yes" questions, he would have discovered her lost condition before they dated. (See gospel link under resources.)

The Problem of Dating Someone Who Doesn't Agree with Scriptures

Beware of dating someone who believes in Jesus Christ but adheres to unscriptural teachings. For example, Marilee dated a Christian man who attended a Christian church unlike her own. They married but lived on different spiritual levels. They believed different views on biblical issues. Arguments over biblical issues hindered the stability of their marriage.

Risks of Dating Someone on a Different Spiritual Path

Many Christian couples without similar spiritual direction may marry, believing they are equally united. Unfortunately, after the couple marries, they realize they lack similar spiritual objectives, so their relationship is spiritually lopsided. Difficulties and challenges in marriage are unavoidable, but spiritually mismatched spouses have increased tensions and conflicts.

Sometime after marrying, Judy realized she was unequally united with a believer who didn't have the same spiritual interests. He's slowly, spiritually growing because he is hearing God's Word at church, but he isn't the spiritual leader in the home. He sometimes interrupts her Bible reading time, has excuses for neglecting Bible reading, or doesn't lead devotions or pray about decisions. Judy frequently feels compelled to serve the Lord in some special way, which her husband can't understand.

Elliot had a rude awakening when he realized that he married a believer who had a different spiritual perspective. She liked to go to church with him, but reading the Word of God and praying as a couple didn't interest her. He shared his faith with others, but she criticized when he witnessed to their friends. Elliot enjoys evangelism with the church group, but his wife whines or protests with pointless remarks.

Lynn, unequally united spiritually with her believer husband, suffers frequent disappointments. Whenever she listens to Christian music, he makes faultfinding comments and leaves the room. When they visit with others, and she talks about Christ, he questions why she said that. Involvement at church interests her, but he criticizes or puts obstacles in her way. He won't go to church with her, but he says he is a believer. Now Lynn wonders if he is unsaved or just a carnal believer. Since her husband isn't the spiritual leader, Lynn has no sense of security or feeling of protection.

What should a spiritually unequally united spouse do? The spiritually minded spouse should continue to hear and read the Word of God, pray for her spouse, and obey God's marriage commands of love and respect. The believer husband displays *agape* love even if the wife doesn't deserve love. Similarly, a believer wife obeys by demonstrating *agape* love, which includes unconditionally respecting her husband, even if he is unworthy of respect. The Christ-centered spouse will continue to find joy and fulfillment in Jesus Christ—the sweetness that covers all sorrows and disappointments.

The Struggles of Dating a Carnal Believer

Believers can become confused and date a carnal believer (a believer whose conduct and flaws don't reflect a relationship with the Lord). A carnal Christian follows his sin nature (flesh/self-will) instead of the Holy Spirit.

How to Recognize a Carnal Believer

A carnal man might take control and make decisions without regard for the woman. For example, Greg announces to Meg, "I decided that God's will is that you should be my wife. So we will get married right away."

Some basics about a carnal Christian include:

- √ The carnal person revolves around "self."

- √ A carnal believer may have addictions to alcohol or drugs, obsessions with pornography or other fixations, or behave abusively.

- √ Carnal believers are disapproving, have problems with anger, or display other traits that don't represent living for Christ.

God commands us to withdraw from believers who are following their lust. *"In the name of the Lord Jesus Christ, we command you, brothers, to keep away from every brother who is idle and does not live according to the teaching you received from us"* (2 Thessalonians 3:6 NIV). Be careful about those with whom you date and the people with whom they associate. Women who have low self-worth from being shamed and abused often gravitate towards the wrong type of man because they feel they don't deserve any better.

> *The chains of sin are too light to be felt until*
> *they are so strong you cannot break them.*
>
> —CBZ

How to Recognize Abuse in Your Dating Experience

Abuse can begin in Christian marriages, but the warning signs are often present before marriage. Since abuse can occur while dating, know the warning signs, and don't ignore or rationalize them.

How Does Your Date Treat You?

Check for gentleness or harshness in the tone of voice—no *snapping* at someone. Also, pay attention to body language that may suggest impatience instead of compassion and tenderness. Potential harm includes alcohol or drug addictions, and abusive behaviors.

Abuse manifests itself as cruel, rude, and coercion used to maintain power or control over another. Abuse is the improper treatment of something or someone; to treat cruelly or violently, especially regularly or repeatedly; to treat unfairly, roughly or improperly for one's gain or satisfaction. Besides physical abuse, other forms of abuse would include psychological, emotional, verbal, sexual, or financial.

Key points to consider are:

> ➤ The severity of the hurt or injury.

> ➤ The overall context of the relationship is a determination of abuse.

> ➤ Does a particular incident increase the degree of abuse? But in other cases, it doesn't.

> ➤ Is the repeated negative behavior part of the general pattern?

How do abusers view themselves?

> √ They think they can behave the way they want.

> √ They believe they can get away with it.

√ They have learned that they can get what they want.

√ They believe they are more important than others are.

What Are Some Warning Signs of Abuse?

By identifying the early warning signs of abuse, you'll avoid entering risky dating or you'll leave a destructive dating experience. The following abusive traits apply to both men and women:

Controlling behavior. Questions whom you talk to and where you go, checks your cell phone or email without your permission, tells you what to do, or uses sulking or manipulation to control or dominate

Quick involvement. Claims "I've never loved anyone as I love you," pressures for exclusive commitment too soon after meeting.

Pressures. May coerce you for sexual favors.

Jealousy. Excessive possessiveness; calls or texts constantly; visits unexpectedly, which demonstrates insecurity.

Unrealistic expectations. Expects you to say or act perfect according to expectations.

Possessiveness. Tries to keep you away from your family or friends.

Blaming behavior. Falsely accuses you or others, blames others for his own mistakes. Doesn't take responsibility for her feelings. "You made me angry" or blames your behavior for his negative feelings or abusive actions.

Hypersensitivity. Feelings easily hurt, will rant about injustices that are normal life experiences. Looks for fights, blows issues out of proportion.

Cruel. Disrespectful or spiteful.

Verbal abuse. Constantly putting you down, insulting you, name-calling.

Rigid gender roles. The man who expects you to serve and obey him whenever he demands it, thinks women are inferior to men, needs a relationship to feel whole.

Sudden mood swings. Can switch from calm to anger or happy to sad in a couple of minutes.

Admits to battering. Admits striking women but justifies it, saying they or the situation provoked it; physically hurts you; believes women dominate by hitting a man.

Threatens violence. A man might say, "I'll break your neck" and then dismisses it with "I didn't mean it."

Uses violence for gain. To punish you, he breaks your special possessions, beats fist on the table, and throws items at or near you.

Explosive temper. Has little or no self-control and wants his way.

Do You Know How to Identify Harmful Flaws?

A couple needs time alone together to test the genuine nature of another since people are usually on their best behavior among others.

Alone time with the one you are dating can help you:

- √ Recognize flaws and behaviors that are intolerable.

- √ Identify whether someone is living for the Lord and desires to follow God's will.

- √ Discover what you like or dislike about a person.

- √ Check if he or she poses potential harm.

- √ Identify a player (a manipulator who pretends to care but is only interested in selfish desires) or a noncommittal individual.

- √ Recognize ambivalence.

Other potential warning signals include mental illness (even among Christians) and neurological disorders, which can suggest future problems. Don't try to rescue those with problems. You aren't responsible for solving the problems of others; however, pray for them.

How Will You Protect Yourself from Abuse?

The regular, repeated patterns of these behaviors indicate abuse. Know the signs so you can protect yourself and leave the dating relationship. Since you cannot change the abuser or the abuser's behavior, don't date that person. Don't ignore the abuse or excuse it, and tell a trusted friend or relative about the abuse. Your responsibility excludes trying to change the abuser because no one can change another. The behavior of another is never your fault; each person chooses to sin. Praying for others is always God's will.

Are You Willing to Break a Harmful Association?

Individuals who crave attention will date anyone who shows them attention or affection. Christians may feel trapped or guilty about dating someone they know is wrong for them.

Read Megan's compelling story.

> Growing up I struggled with acceptance, so I looked for attention, especially from the opposite sex. When I was 16, I started dating, Chuck, an unbeliever. I knew it wasn't the

Lord's will to date him, but I desperately wanted his affection, which I thought was love.

Over the next several years, I grew dissatisfied with my relationship with Chuck, but at the same time felt trapped. Questions would plague my mind. Will I ever find someone else? If I break up with him, won't I feel lonely and depressed? Despite these questions, I knew the Lord was drawing me to Him. I prayed that He would break us up because I was too weak to break it off.

One day Chuck came home from a men's conference he had attended. He told me he had something that he needed to tell me. I nervously asked him what it was and he admitted he had struggled with a pornography obsession for years. I was crushed. Didn't he love me? Didn't he know how much this would hurt me? The next several months were immensely difficult for me emotionally, and I struggled with body image. I had prayed to get out of the relationship. Finally, I broke it off, which was difficult. I felt so relieved and free.

A broken relationship led me to my Savior's loving arms, a place where God loves me unconditionally and forgives my shortcomings. I knew the only person to run to was Christ. Despite some struggles and distractions following this relationship, my Savior comforted me. He was faithful to me.

The Lord later blessed me with a sweet husband who wants to serve the Lord. We desire that our marriage would focus on Christ, and although this is not always so, the Lord remains faithful and brings us joy in Himself. Through the trials He carried me, and I discovered true joy, completeness, and purpose only in Him.

It is better to ask the Lord to direct your paths than to correct your mistakes.

—CBZ

A woman probably won't discover a pornography obsession through dating. Also, a man obsessed with this may find freedom from—and partly through—marriage. Present your Christian qualities, which may attract a possible grace-oriented, Christ-centered Christian spouse. Then leave the matter in the Lord's sovereign hands to direct your life.

*Keep your eyes wide open before marriage
and half shut afterward.*

Study Questions

Use Scripture verses when you can.

1. Give reasons why a believer should not date an unbeliever?

2. Describe how a believer can determine whether someone is a true believer.

3. Name some hazards of marrying an unsaved person.

4. How do some *believers* who date become unequally united in marriage?

5. What have you learned about dating a carnal believer?

6. Why should there be scriptural agreement when you are dating?

7. What helpful things did you learn about an abusive person?

8. What did you learn about protecting yourself while dating?

9. What was the most valuable information you learned from this chapter?

CHAPTER 9

How to Be Faithful to Your Future Spouse

What constitutes cheating on your future spouse?
Have you heard of secondary virginity?
What can you do to protect your future?

In this chapter you will read about:

- ♥ The costs of promiscuity and God's comfort after sin

- ♥ Secondary virginity

- ♥ How to defeat the obsession with sexual immorality

- ♥ Gaining respect, confidence, and contentment to protect your future

I Was Promiscuous—What Hope Is There for Me?

Hunter asks,

> In my youth I was promiscuous. When God convicted me of my sin of sexual immorality, I admitted it to God, and He forgave me. I repented (a biblical term meaning to "change one's mind") about my lifestyle of promiscuity and began a life of *secondary virginity*. My desire to obey God's commands

gave me peace in Christ. Praise God who rescued me from the powerful and destructive lifestyle of promiscuity!

Since then I have been reading, hearing, and applying God's Word to my life. Even though I have been practicing abstinence for years, my past creates a conflict with Christy, a Christian woman I'm dating. She has remained morally pure and hoped to marry a pure man.

Hunter's honesty with Christy is commendable since he could have concealed his past and hoped it would never surface. Since Hunter has been living a life of secondary virginity for years and guarding his close relationship with the Lord, he has proven himself trustworthy. Nevertheless, his past is a serious concern. Before further dates with Hunter, Christy must settle issues including "will she be able to trust him."

We could compare the recovery of a promiscuous person to an alcoholic who stopped drinking. Initially, those around him fear he will resume drinking. Although recovery from drinking isn't easy, it is possible, especially for a Christian depending on the Lord for victory. Each day the alcoholic abstains, the craving for alcohol lessens until it disappears and a new lifestyle emerges. People associated with the recovering alcoholic begin to trust the individual's sobriety as the days and years pass. Similarly, the same pattern of trust can develop for the formerly promiscuous individual who has been living a secondary virginity lifestyle.

If individuals would consider that promiscuity means cheating on their future spouse or with someone else's, less heartache, suffering, and broken relationships would result.

> *God takes care of his children even if they are*
> *disobedient, but they will have to suffer consequences.*

What Comfort Does Scripture Offer the Sinner?

Once a believer admits her sin to God the Father, He forgives it and forgets it. *"As far as the east is from the west, So far has He removed our transgressions* [sins] *from us"* (Psalm 103:12). If your conscience causes guilt to linger, think of the promise of 1 John 1:9, that God is faithful to forgive your confessed sin. *"If we are faithless, He remains faithful; He cannot deny Himself"* (2 Timothy 2:13). Since God forgives you and forgets your sin (Psalm 32:1), so forgive yourself, and then continue your life in obedience to Him.

> *God forgives sin and casts it in the ocean,*
> *then He places a "No Fishing" sign.*

How did Christ handle the sin of the adulterous woman? Christ confronted an adulterous woman at a Samaritan well (John 4:4-26). He helped the woman see her sin and admit it, but He didn't focus on her sin. Instead, He drew attention to Himself as her Savior from sin, and she received Him as her personal Savior. What a magnificent face-to-face meeting with her Savior!

Since God always forgives us, He asks that we also forgive each other. Forgiveness doesn't cling to the hurt. Instead, true forgiveness moves forward, not calling for retribution or behaving unloving toward the sinner because of his sin.

> *We forgive others as long as Christ forgives us!*

If a believer can't forgive the confessed sin of another, it's possible she thinks herself better than another. *"For by the grace given me I say to every one of you: Do not think of yourself more highly than you ought, but rather think of yourself with sober judgment, in accordance with the measure of God has given you"* (Romans 12:3 NIV). If the Christian can't forgive someone's sin, maybe he is guilty of the sin of pride.

> *When the believer is unforgiving, he's out of fellowship*
> *with God the Father, so he spiritually harms himself.*

Consider what Corrie ten Boom said about forgiveness.

Corrie ten Boom likens forgiveness to letting go of a bell rope. If you have ever seen a country church with a bell in the steeple, you will remember that to get the bell ringing, you have to tug awhile. Once it has begun to ring, you merely maintain the momentum. As long as you keep pulling, the bell keeps ringing.

Corrie ten Boom says forgiveness is letting go of the rope. It is just that simple, but when you do so, the bell keeps ringing. Momentum is still at work. However, if you keep your hands off the rope, the bell will begin to slow and eventually stop.

It is like that with forgiveness. When you decide to forgive, the old feelings of unforgiveness may continue to assert themselves. After all, they have lots of momentum. But if you affirm your decision to forgive, that unforgiving spirit will begin to slow and will eventually be still. Forgiveness is letting go of the "rope" of retribution.

—*Encyclopedia of 15,000 Illustrations:*
Signs of the Times

In His love, God forgives you and forgets about your sin.
Dare we not follow His example of loving
and forgiving another?

How Serious Are the Consequences of Promiscuity?

In our Satan-controlled culture, sexual sin isn't only permitted; it's promoted. Satan's deception is that sexual sin outside marriage is just another acceptable activity that everyone does. But God commands, *"Beloved, I beg you as sojourners and pilgrims, abstain from fleshly lusts which war against the soul"* (1 Peter 2:11). *"Flee also youthful lusts; but pursue righteousness, faith, love, peace with those who call on the Lord out of a pure heart"* (2 Timothy 2:22). In this godless world, have we forgotten that our heavenly Father, who created sex, knows better than we do? God promises to reward those who trust Him by remaining pure (Hebrews 11:25-26 NIV).

While God frequently delays negative consequences of our reaping what we sow, He pledges, *"Do not be deceived, God is not mocked; for whatever a man sows, that he will also reap. For he who sows to his flesh will of the flesh reap corruption, but he who sows to the Spirit will of the Spirit reap everlasting life"* (Galatians 6:7-8). Although God always forgives our confessed sin, we must live with the consequences of sin—even forgiven sin. Though a believer can never lose his salvation (John 10:28-30), he will suffer the harvest of his sin on earth, i.e., "we reap what we sow" (Galatians 6:7-8). Also, at the judgment seat of Christ, believers will give an account of their failures to depend on God. So there will be shame for sowing to fleshly desires (1 John 2:28). But the believer who sows to please the Spirit reaps the life of Christ manifested in his life.

Unfortunately, the media and those in authority rarely warn against the consequences of prohibited sex. Individuals may forget or disregard their sins, but the damage of their sins will follow them. Although God forgives confessed sin, the harmful price of sin hurts both the offender and others. For example, Jacob who deceived, later was deceived (Genesis 27-29); Ahab and Jezebel paid with their lives for their deception (1 Kings 21). The adulterous sin of King David with Bathsheba (2 Samuel 11:1-13) led to the murder of her husband, Uriah (11:14-27). Also, the consequences to David personally, to his family, and to the nation of Israel were devastating (See remainder of 2 Samuel).

Sin would have few takers
if its results occurred immediately.

—CBZ

Can You Afford the Price of Promiscuity?

1. Sexual sins affect your entire being. These sins cause emotional, physical, and spiritual harm. *"Flee sexual immorality. Every sin that a man* *does is outside the body, but he who commits sexual immorality sins against his own body"* (1 Corinthians 6:18).

Sexual sin hurts emotionally. These sins manipulate the feelings into slavery to that sin (1 Corinthians 6:12b). Sexual activity with another always causes a joining of the souls. Emotional bonding occurs, and when the couple separates, emotional pain results. With every sexual encounter and breakup, intimate memories, hurts, and other feelings remain. Each person leaves a part of his soul behind. Also, promiscuous individuals usually suffer guilt, self-loathing, shame, regrets, and depression—and they may withdraw from people.

Promiscuity injures physically. In addition to reaping emotional pain is the risk of STDs—sexually transmitted diseases that God's Word warns about in 1 Corinthians 6:18. Millions are reaping the damages of venereal diseases, reaching widespread prevalence, along with an alarming increase in mental disorders. How painful to watch sensuality grip people and degrade their entire life by enslaving them to sinful habits that destroy.

> *The sin of one person often brings tragedy to many.*
> —CBZ

Sexual sin harms spiritual wellness. God gave principles and rules of purity to shield us from harm and misery. However, breaking God's principles produces emotional suffering and spiritual bondage. The devastation of guilt and shame causes individuals to wish for death and others to question whether they are saved. How Christ's heart must ache to see His beloved, blood-bought child reaping self-inflicted misery!

The promiscuous Christian loses fellowship with God and the blessings associated with it. How can a believer living outside the will of God experience joy in the Lord? Abandoning God's will grieves the Holy Spirit and hinders Him from working the life of Christ through the believer. Is the pleasure of sin worth this great price?

> *The most miserable people are carnal Christians.*

2. Sexual immorality forfeits trust. We may be able to forgive, but we can't immediately trust that person, and trust may never return. Trust isn't the same as forgiveness; trust must be earned. A promiscuous single is unfaithful to a future spouse. Therefore, when promiscuous singles marry, their past unfaithfulness often becomes an obstacle to a good marriage. Since impurity damages trust, doubt increases questions: "Since she was promiscuous and didn't wait for marriage, will she be faithful during the marriage?" Because of past relationships, each person may wonder if he or she can trust the spouse. "Will he be comparing me to previous partners?" Such disturbing concerns can deepen when problems arise in the marriage.

3. Sexual sin will cost you your Christian testimony. Sadly, our culture increasingly accepts promiscuity. Even Christian parents, relatives, and friends now tolerate promiscuity and say nothing to their loved ones about the sinful behavior. A believer's promiscuity causes heartache for parents and others who adhere to the principles of Scripture, yet they won't confront.

Additionally, other believers live through intense sorrow and distress because this sin hinders the gospel of Christ. Christians should set examples of living for Christ and promoting the gospel; instead, they hinder their Christian witness with the unsaved because of sinful conduct. Our Father is concerned about our conduct because how we behave may affect how others respond to Christ (Matthew 5:16; Colossians 4:5-6; 2 Timothy 2:22-26; Titus 2:1-8; 1 Peter 3:15-16).

> *The conduct of individual members of the body of Christ harms the spiritual well-being of the entire church.*

4. Promiscuity will cost you your reputation. Despite disagreements about what constitutes morality, people agree adultery is wrong. Though promiscuous behavior takes place in secret, people will find out; sometimes a premarital pregnancy reveals impurity. People will not forget even if they do forgive. Although the stigma isn't as strong as in the past, in God's eyes this sinful behavior is serious.

What Lies about Promiscuity Do Couples Believe?

Many people believe Satan's lie that sex will help you keep your boyfriend or girlfriend. Or this enticement: "If you love me, you will do this." You could reply, "If you love me, you'll wait." Satan's deceptions promise pleasure, but he never tells you the troubles that sin creates.

Lust cannot wait. True love chooses to wait.

Satan's deceit broadcasts that living together before marriage is acceptable, but doesn't disclose the costs. But, consider that most single couples who live together never marry each other and those who do marry have a higher divorce rate. For some, an engagement ring encourages a subtle lie—"We're married in God's sight, and we are committed for life, so why wait?" The engagement period isn't a license for sexual intimacy, but a marriage license is. Marriage requires discipline including sexual discipline. If you can't practice restraint during the engagement, you may have problems in the marriage.

How People Pervert God's Marriage Design

Many who practice promiscuity don't know or choose to disobey God's plan for marriage. Since God designed sexual intimacy for marriage only, in any other context the purpose of sex is perverted, and the Lord is dishonored. How can I'm-engaged sex, co-habiting sex, one-time sex, casual sex, or recreational sex honor God? Do you see how non-marital sex defiles, cheapens and dishonors God and His marriage plan?

Wickedness never goes unpunished;
righteousness never goes unrewarded.

—CBZ

As stated previously, God designed marriage as the union of one man and one woman for life (Genesis 2:18-24). Why do you suppose that God created woman from man and not from dust, as He created man? He fashioned woman from the man's flesh and bone to depict marriage of a man and woman as one flesh. The goal of marriage should be more than friendship; it should be one of unity, of oneness. Marriage is a cherished union of the couples' hearts and minds. Throughout Scriptures, God takes this special union seriously. God designed sex as intimate physical communication of love between a man and a woman in marriage. According to God's Word, the only sex that glorifies God is marital.

How to Think Clearly While Dating

If a dating couple knows each other apart from sexual activity, they'll be able to make an intelligent decision whether to marry. But if a dating couple is promiscuous, the focus is physical; the couple overlooks important flaws or fails to know the person on a deeper, intellectual level. Also, premarital sex alters the bonding and trust processes necessary for a successful marriage, and thus, another reason for a high divorce rate.

As noted earlier, God warns us three times through Solomon's book of Songs not to "arouse or awaken love before its time" (Song of Songs 2:7). Solomon waited or abstained so he could give himself to his bride.

Travis (a believer who was 28 before he married) had unsaved friends who questioned him, "Travis, what do you do about sex?" His response was, "I wait!" His amazed friends couldn't imagine him that old and sexually inactive. Travis followed God's will, denying his fleshly longings. Since Travis avoided tempting circumstances where he would be alone with a woman, he was untroubled and relaxed. God honors waiting!

Your peers may prod and push you to yield to your desires. Fight back with Scripture. *"And do not be conformed to this world, but be transformed by the renewing of your mind, that you may prove what is that good and acceptable and perfect will of God"* (Romans 12:2). Yielding to God's way is evidence that you choose to live for Christ, not self. Respect yourself and your standards by setting boundaries. Let your date know your high-values, so she or he will respect you.

Trusting God and His standards provide confidence in the circumstances and causes others to respect us.

What Can You Do to Protect Your Future?

Find a balance between being with others and alone while dating. Spend time getting to know each other's friends and parents at dinner or activities with them. Get to know each other by talking with each other on the phone, at a restaurant, or taking a walk.

Plan your dates around wholesome activities. Enjoy bowling, tennis, softball, archery, paintball, or skating; indoor sports complexes offer other sports. Other fun activities may include God-pleasing concerts, art galleries, museums, a stage play, ballroom dancing, taking a class together, visiting a botanical garden, church gatherings, or playing board games. For more conversation time, you could stop at a restaurant after an activity.

Also, avoid questionable places or situations where Christian singles should not spend time. *"Do not be deceived: 'Bad company corrupts good morals'"* (1 Corinthians 15:33 NASB). Even carnal Christians can lead other believers astray. Use the car for travel to your date, not for the date itself. Avoid being alone in private settings where temptations may increase.

> One of the reasons we yield to temptations is that we are like the little boy in the pantry. His mother heard a noise because he had taken down the cookie jar. She said, "Willie, where are you?" He answered that he was in the pantry. "What are you doing there?" He said, "I'm fighting temptation." My friend, that is not the place to fight temptation! That is the place to start running.
>
> —J. Vernon McGee,
> *Thru the Bible!*

How to Find Confidence and Contentment

Even though we know Satan's offer doesn't satisfy, sin may be temporarily fun. Seeking to satisfy needs their way, Christians abandon God's will. Pornography often traps boys and men. Girls and women may compromise their morals and forfeit their virginity to find love. A woman who gives in sexually can dissuade a man from wanting to marry—he already has what he wanted.

Individuals who need fulfillment are failing to depend on the Lord to their meet needs. Instead, they look for a quick fix to gratify the sin nature (flesh self) and indulge in pleasures of Satan's world. Instead of finding true peace, they feel discontented, frustrated, and anxious.

God promises something better—contentment. *"Be anxious for nothing, but in everything by prayer and supplication with thanksgiving let your requests be made known to God.? And the peace of God, which surpasses all comprehension, will guard your hearts and your minds in Christ Jesus"* (Philippians 4:6-7 NASB). God doesn't promise to meet your needs immediately or even give you what you ask.

God's peace awaits those who wait on Him to meet their needs in His perfect way and timing. Our heavenly Father knows our needs and desires. *"If you then, being evil, know how to give good gifts to your children, how much more will your Father who is in heaven give what is good to those who ask Him!"* (Matthew 7:11 NASB). Will you trust our sovereign God to provide His best for you at the right time, whether He gives the gift of singleness or marriage?

> *Those who see God's hand in everything*
> *can best leave everything in God's hand.*
>
> —CBZ

Study Questions

When possible, quote Scripture to back up your answers.

1. What comfort does Scripture give to the sinner?

2. How often should we forgive someone?

3. How does premarital sex distress a relationship?

4. Although a believer cannot lose his salvation, what does Scripture tell us about sin in Galatians 6:7 and 1 John 2:28?

5. List the high costs of promiscuity.

6. Marriage requires _____, including sexual discipline. If you can't practice _____ restraint during engagement, you may have problems in marriage.

7. According to Scripture, only _____ sex glorifies God.

8. What are ways to protect your future while dating?

9. How can you display respect, confidence, and contentment while dating?

CHAPTER 10

What You Need to Know about Flirting

**What is flirting?
Isn't flirting innocent and acceptable?
Do you know the dangers and subtle pitfalls of flirting?**

This chapter will:

- ♥ Describe and identify flirting.

- ♥ Examine the dangers of flirting.

- ♥ Provide biblical perspectives.

Why You Should Be Cautious of Flirting

A missionary friend offered the following observations about flirting.

> As a missionary in Asia and learning their cultures, I learned about my western culture and me. After living in one area a few months, I heard them talking about *playing* with eyes between male and female. My curiosity caused me to ask what that meant and if my missionary partner or I ever did that. They told me that my partner did it sometimes, but I did it more. I was appalled when I realized they considered direct eye contact with a grin and maybe a joke as flirting.

I began to think about the way my culture and I freely joke and tease between the sexes. I realized that sometimes flirting was a way of getting and giving attention that boosted the ego. I also learned that flirting could initiate a personal or even intimate relationship without realizing it.

Several years later after I married, the Lord convicted me that my conduct was a sin. I liked the ego boost that fed my flesh and was possibly giving a wrong impression. In faith, I committed to guarding against this.

Question: What does the Bible say about flirting?

Answer: Since the Bible doesn't specifically say flirting is wrong, we should examine the definition of flirting. According to Merriam-Webster, "flirting is (a) to behave amorously without serious intent or (b) to show superficial or casual interest or liking." Flirting is synonymous with the word *trifle*, something of little value. Next, we examine what people usually try to accomplish when they flirt. Are they seeking negative or positive attention from others? Are they trying to show sexual interest or attraction? Do they see it as innocent fun, whether a person is involved with someone else or even married?

Although many people think that as long as nothing happens physically, what happens in our minds is irrelevant. But God denounces it. *"But I say, anyone who even looks at a woman with lust in his eye has already committed adultery with her in his heart."* (Matthew 5:28).

Sin begins in our minds. *"Let no one say when he is tempted, 'I am tempted by God;' for God cannot be tempted by evil, nor does He Himself tempt anyone. But each one is tempted when he is drawn away by his own desires and enticed. Then, when desire has conceived, it gives birth to sin; and sin, when it is full-grown, brings forth death"* (James 1:13-15). Whatever we surround ourselves with, whatever we indulge ourselves in, and whatever we fill our minds with influences what we will become. Matthew 12:35 reminds us that *"a good person produces good words from a good heart, and an evil person produces evil words from an evil heart."* Philippians 4:8 commands, "Fix your thoughts on what is true and honorable and right. Think about things that are pure and lovely and admirable. Think about things that are excellent and worthy of praise."

Although people usually describe flirting as harmless, it rarely, if ever, is. Consider what people think about those who flirt. A woman who habitually flirts, for example, can acquire a promiscuous reputation. She will find that other women look at her as a threat and take an instant disliking to her. A man who often flirts gains the reputations of a womanizer. A habitual flirt enjoys the attention, but people don't respect a flirt.

God expects examples that show others the love of Christ through our behavior (Ephesians 5:1-2). When a man or woman struggles with lustful thoughts, a flirt will add to their distress. When a person of the opposite sex hangs on someone, touches, winks, or shows off her body, that behavior causes another's struggle with temptation more difficult. The Bible strongly warns us against tempting others to sin (Matthew 18:7). Instead of tempting unsaved individuals, we should strive to lead them to saving faith in Jesus Christ. Neither should we do anything that would cause believers to falter in their Christian walk (Romans14:21).

This article about flirting was adapted and used with permission from "got questions" at www.gotquestions.org/flirting.html.

How Is Flirting Cheating or Defrauding Another?

Many individuals, including professionals, consider flirting as harmless, amid proper boundaries, with someone outside of marriage. These restrictions vary with each couple. Some people consider flirting inappropriate, and others accept it.

Cyber (computer-generated) communications, including social media sites, now introduce the topic of flirting into discussions frequently. When you interact online, you could unintentionally grow closer to someone. What may appear as just talking could mistakenly appear seductive. Online chatting entices women because they can fulfill their emotional needs sitting at their computer. However, seemingly harmless cyber friendships often develop into intense emotional and physical affairs that damage marriages.

No small sin is small because all sin opposes God.
—CBZ

Trey communicated via email with Becky, a married woman. When Luke confronted him, Trey claimed they were just friends. Luke prodded further, "What do you email about? Does she tell you her problems or her marital difficulties?" "Yes," Trey replied adding, "she just wants someone to talk to." Luke questioned, "Don't you see that by confiding in you she is betraying her husband? Becky shouldn't talk with another man about her marriage problems. Trey, do you see how you have come between Becky and her husband? Betrayal is betrayal! Emotional betrayal is as serious as sexual unfaithfulness. Have you ever considered that these seemingly innocent encounters could lead to an affair? Has it?" Trey responded, "No, we're just emailing. I hear what you are saying. I never thought about it that way. Thanks, Luke for taking the time to warn me. It's clear now that I must end this. I don't want to cause a marriage breakup. And I don't want to fight God's will."

*You cannot put your sins behind you
until you are willing to face them.*
—CBZ

How Is Flirting Contradictory to *Agape* Love?

Flirting behavior is frequently sexual. You enter a danger zone if you notice the person with whom you interact feeds your sexual fantasies (affairs often start from sexual fantasy). Beware if conversations contain subtle sexual overtones. Even if you aren't touching each other, your words can be seductive. Guard your friendship with the opposite sex, so it doesn't lead to an affair, even an emotional one. Avoid becoming involved with another through flirting, which shifts focus away from the person you are dating. In essence, flirting can be defrauding since it diverts your feelings and thoughts from another. Flirting may be defrauding, which is contrary to *agape* love.

> *Flirtatious behavior expresses self-interest;*
> *but agape love seeks the best interest of another.*

The Warning Flags of Flirting

1. **Are you spending too much time talking with someone?** Not only do we need to consider the content of messages, but also the time spent communicating. One woman spent three hours every night on Facebook, chatting with her online male friend until she realized that was more time than she spent with her fiancée.

2. **Do we rationalize flirting?** If we engage in innocent non-secretive conversations, then we wouldn't have to explain it by saying, "He's only a friend." A harmless friendship wouldn't need justification. If the friendship appears harmless to both individuals, the relationship is proper conduct (if they aren't deceiving themselves). If you wrestle with guilt or need to rationalize, you may be engaging in a risky friendship.

3. **Does this person meet our personal needs?** Do you find emotional satisfaction with an online friend or with a coworker with whom you flirt? If so, stop and ask "Why?" Another caution: Don't share personal information with others and fail to share personally with someone you're dating, even though that friend understands better.

4. **Does your dating partner dislike this behavior?** Consider your date's disapproval of your conversations with the opposite

sex a warning sign. Is your flirting behavior with another person distracting or hindering your relationship with the person you are dating?

5. **Does a friend voice concern?** Perhaps a good friend questions why you talk so much about this person. Does she caution, "You're engaged." "He's married." "You're dating!" Often mothers, sisters, and friends can see these red flags before a person willingly identifies them.

6. **Are you seeking attention?** Some men find attention from an attractive woman who builds up his ego and tells him that he is "funny," "smart," "sexy." Perhaps you seek an admirer by flirting and provoke jealousy to gain attention from someone else, which might work, but it is manipulation.

*The nearer we are to God, the more conscious
we become of sin.*

—CBZ

Study Questions

Give Scripture references when possible.

1. What is flirting? Give examples of flirting.

2. How is flirting contrary to God's standards?

3. How does flirting defraud someone?

4. How does flirting contradict *agape* love?

CHAPTER 11

Modesty: How Much Are You Compromising?

Do you have questions about modesty?
Is there a difference between modesty and legalism?
Why is modesty important to God?

Today we will:

- ♥ Examine what is and isn't modest dress.

- ♥ Discover why modesty is important to God.

- ♥ how to dress modestly yet fashionable.

- ♥ Discover why modesty should be important in your Christian life.

While this topic is directed toward girls and women, many principles of modesty apply to boys and men. Men who understand modesty may find this information personally helpful since they may need to confront a sister. Many young women don't immodestly dress because they want to be provocative, they simply don't understand what immodest dress looks like and God's command on the matter.

To be clear, I am not legalistic, and I am NOT mandating a particular style of dress. I am merely offering a biblical viewpoint for you to consider (before the Lord) regarding attire.

Scripture states that the main purpose of clothing is a covering for the body. Most people believe this statement is true. But let's look deeper for the truth. In the beginning, Adam and Eve wore no clothing and felt no shame since they were sinless. However, after they sinned, they felt guilt and shame. Therefore, they covered their private body parts with fig leaves, which was their idea of appropriate.

God *did* care what Adam and Eve wore, but He was most concerned with the condition of their hearts. They had disobeyed Him, and therefore, they were out of fellowship with Him. He first dealt with their broken relationship with Him by holding them accountable. Next God provided appropriate clothing for them using animal skin—the first blood sacrifice (Genesis 2–3). However, God had greater concern about the sin barrier between Adam and Eve and Himself. He required payment for sin. In His grace, God knew animal sacrifices were a temporary atonement, but He would eventually need to deal completely with sin at the cross. This, of course, foreshadowed Christ's future coming. Jesus Christ would be God's Lamb who would be sacrificed to cover man's sin with His righteousness. Spiritually speaking, believers wear Christ's robe of righteousness.

God cares most about our heart—the inner self, and He cares about what we wear on the outside. Unfortunately, our culture reveals its idea of covering when they promote "Take it off" or show off your body. But the godly person will willingly submit to God's plan and accept His principles for covering the body. Scripture always refers to nakedness as shameful except in the context of a husband (a man) and wife (a woman) in the privacy of their marriage.

Although the Bible gives us no specifics for acceptable clothing styles, it does give us principles that help us know how best to dress.

Five Biblical Principles to Guide Us

Principle 1
Modesty Is Not Optional; It Is God's Command

> *"I also want women to dress modestly, with decency and propriety, not with braided hair or gold or pearls or expensive clothes, but with good deeds, appropriate for women who profess to worship God"* (1 Timothy 2:9-10 NIV).

As Christians, we represent Christ in every area of our life and at all times. This verse speaks of dressing modestly as one who represents Jesus Christ. Paul was contrasting the artificial glamour of the world with the true beauty of the Christian life.

The term "modest" means "decent and orderly." That biblical word includes the absence of sexual suggestiveness and emphasizes an appearance that is basic, moderate, sensible, and free from ostentation. Paul wasn't forbidding jewelry or lovely clothing. He urged women to dress with decency, orderliness, and in good taste. While it is our Christian liberty to wear jewelry or specific hairstyles, ostentatious attire or accessories, or exaggerated hairstyles can be a distraction from the Christian life. Paul is referring to flamboyant hairstyles, including women exhibiting male haircuts, and unnatural hair colors.

Paul was urging women to emphasize modesty and a godly character, and not look or act like the world around them. Our appearance ought to reflect the beauty of our magnificent Savior, not the world's values.

> *Modesty is not really about clothing, guys, or your body.*
> *It's about Jesus, and we need to be glorifying Him*
> *in everything we do—including how we dress.*
>
> —Emily Susanne

What I wear is no one's business but mine. I should have the freedom to wear what I choose. That statement is false. As we have seen, dress matters to God, and it is His business how we represent Him.

Since Christians are under grace and not Law, they may dress however they please. So it would be legalistic to have a dress code? Those statements are *false* and *true*. To make modesty a rule to dress a certain way, or to emphasize a particular way of dress or the importance of the way a believer should dress, could be legalistic (adherence to rules). Modestly dressing doesn't have to be legalistic since what you wear ought to come from an attitude of "what would please my Savior." A Christian woman who dresses immodestly is forgetting that she is an ambassador of the One who redeemed her. *"For you were bought at a price; therefore glorify God in your body and in your spirit, which are God's"* (1 Corinthians 6:20).

Should we let our children should choose for themselves how to dress? Perhaps you aren't sure. Kids, teens, and even young adults may need guidance and direction from their parents, pastors, and church leaders in the area of modesty. If we don't teach biblical principles of dress to children, how will they learn? Parents must not allow their children to mimic the ungodly people. How a mom models modesty in conduct or appearance will influence her daughter more than what she may say. Husbands and fathers have the responsibility of enforcing modesty. We must train our children, girls and boys, about modesty of conduct and appearance (Eph. 6:4). Training children to love God and want to obey Him, then applying principles to modesty is not legalism.

Obeying God's command to be modest is not a question of legalism or dress code. It's a question of obedience with a proper heart attitude, which exalts our Savior. Some may see obedience as a burden or duty, instead of a means to blessing. (1 John 5:3). But, God always gives His best to those who follow His will. Spirituality (living by faith) comes first, which results in obedience. However, man's way is to obey from our flesh to become spiritual, which is backward. Consider how this applies to modesty.

> *Modesty begins with your heart and*
> *then affects what you wear.*

Principle 2
Believers in Jesus Christ Are the Temple of God

> *"Or do you not know that your body is the temple of the Holy Spirit who is in you, whom you have from God, and you are not your own?"* (1 Corinthians 6:19).

We do not belong to ourselves but God. Since God bought us back with the price of Christ's blood, we ought to praise Him with our body and our will. Like a pearl in a shell, a woman's *outer shell* should reflect Christ from an overflow of a heart seeking to glorify Him.

Our appearance, including our clothing, communicates our character, values, and beliefs. We communicate nonverbally through our clothes and appearance. Immodest clothing can contradict our Christian beliefs, our moral values, and our character. If my clothing choices *reflect* what I *believe* then what *beliefs* do my clothing choices *reflect*?

> *When we respect our temple, we are more likely to dress*
> *modestly to reflect Christ and, thus be ready for service*
> *to God and others.*

Principle 3
Modest Appearance Demonstrates *Agape* Love

> *"A new commandment I give to you, that you love one another; as I have loved you, that you also love one another"* (John 13:34).

Remember that *agape* love is doing what is best for another in light of eternity despite what it may cost you. What does *agape* love have to do with modesty?

Some people reason that particular clothing styles are neither right nor wrong; it's just a matter of personal taste or opinion. However, clothing is *not* a matter of taste or opinion, but *it is a matter of what is right or wrong*. Ask yourself, "What am I trying to "say" or what response am I looking for by my choice of clothing?" "Am I causing another to stumble spiritually?"

Others think it's not my problem if a guy struggles morally because of my clothing. The guys are responsible for controlling their minds. Perhaps you don't believe you have a responsibility in the way you dress. Sight arouses men, but women are aroused more by feeling. Males are not alone in the battle against lust. The number of women, even Christian women, visiting porn sites or having sexual fantasies is increasing, together with other perversions. But God says, *"You were taught, with regard to your former way of life, to put off your old self, which is being corrupted by its deceitful desires"* (Ephesians 4:22 NIV). Many women are intentionally enticing men to sin. Therefore, men must find strength in God's standards and principles to live by faith (Galatians 5:16).

Immodest or provocative clothing represent flirtation. Words synonymous with flirtatious dress include sexy, alluring, provocative, or suggestive. Is flirtatious clothing an indication of insecurity or perhaps a sign that the woman doesn't have self-respect? Next time you are tempted to flirt with dress or behavior consider: "Can I wear this or do this to the glory of God?" *"Therefore, whether you eat or drink, or whatever you do, do all to the glory of God"* (1 Corinthians 10:31).

Putting yourself first by seeking attention, tempting someone, or being an obstacle to someone's spiritual life is a failure to display *agape* love.

Christians who present themselves modestly,
demonstrate love to others, which gives glory to Christ.

Principle 4
God Commands Us to Be Lights in This Dark World

*"For you were once darkness,
but now you are light in the Lord.
Live as children of light"* (Ephesians 5:8 NIV).

The world around us pushes us to conform, and many believers are compromising. Movies, TV, and peer pressure have been influential in convincing women to dress a bit revealing if they want men to notice them. Most women in our society think this is true? However, this is *false*. Immodesty draws attention to your body, which men can be guilty of also.

*Modesty isn't as much about how much skin
you aren't showing, but what you say by
what you wear and how you act.*

Is it true that most men don't notice what a woman wears, except for perverts or sex addicts? This statement is false. Most Christian girls and woman don't understand that immodest dress does affect *all* men in general.

> One man believed that he understands that an attractive young lady provocatively dresses because she is seeking the attention of a specific handsome, young man. But in doing so, she is also drawing the attention of ALL the men, both single and married. Her body has become a billboard to ALL of them. And when men look at her advertisements, she thinks THEY are the perverts! How absurd! She is the one doing the advertising!

Being lights in a dark world is equivalent to God's command in Romans 12:2. *"Do not be conformed to this world, but be transformed by the renewing of your minds, so that you may discern what is the will of God—what is good and acceptable and perfect"* (Romans 12:2). We need to avoid making excuses that hinder us from promoting the highest standard of living, namely Christ.

Furthermore, *"But you are a chosen generation, a royal priesthood, a holy nation, His own special people, that you may proclaim the praises of Him who called you out of darkness into His marvelous light"* (1 Peter 2:9). God calls believers a holy nation because we are set apart from sin unto God by our position in Christ. We live *in* the world but must not be a part *of* its standards, regardless of how we feel or how inconvenient it is.

> *The goal of modesty is not merely*
> *to prevent guys from lusting.*
> *The goal of modesty is to reflect inward dignity,*
> *respect for ourselves as God's daughters,*
> *and a desire to obey His command to live set-apart lives.*

Principle 5
God Desires Living Sacrifices

"Therefore, I urge you, brothers, in view of God's mercy, to offer your bodies as living sacrifices, holy and pleasing to God—this is your spiritual act of worship" (Romans 12:1 NIV).

"You also, as living stones, are being built up a spiritual house, a holy priesthood, to offer up spiritual sacrifices acceptable to God through Jesus Christ" (1 Peter 2:5).

As believer priests, we offer our entire life as a living sacrifice. The body represents life and activities, and your body is the means of expression. By choosing to follow principles of modesty, we present a spiritual, living sacrifice to God. The living sacrifice of modesty is a pleasing spiritual act of worship.

*A modest Christian woman offers a living sacrifice
by choosing God's will over our own.*

True, a girl or woman can wear modest clothes and still be immodest. How? Modesty refers to more than just clothing. Modesty includes:

- The way we walk or move.

- The way we talk.

- The way we sit.

- The way we act.

- The way we use our eyes.

- The way we engage with other people, including touch.

- The body language, which can speak volumes to a man.

Immodesty includes suggestive or enticing speech such as blunt and flirtatious comments. Biblical modesty reflects the principles and standards of Christ, not only in your choice of clothing but also in your words and conduct.

In our culture, many think that you cannot be fashionable *and* modest, which is incorrect. When a woman's modesty reveals her true beauty, she is attractive and pleasing. Modesty is something good—a treasure to be protected and cherished.

*Modesty is more than just a hemline; it is an interior
disposition that influences not only our dress
but our thoughts and our actions.*
—Leah Darrow

The Benefits of Modesty

Most girls and women have little understanding of the meaning of modesty, its power, or its benefits. Some girls/women mistakenly think that dressing immodestly is okay. However, men who favor modesty may be hesitant to talk to a woman who dresses provocatively. On the other hand, a modestly dressed Christian woman may have the opportunity to share the gospel with anyone.

Immodest appearance will distract some men, and they may feel uncomfortable to approach such a woman. Immodest dress makes it difficult for a man to see that woman as a believer in Christ. He has a constant battle while talking to a provocative woman. True communication becomes almost impossible. As he tries to listen, he is simultaneously fighting temptation. Men worth meeting and dating aren't interested in a woman they cannot trust, which is what provocative clothing communicates. Men report that an immodestly dressed woman gives the impression that she may not be trustworthy, that she may not make a good wife. Men worth knowing want modestly dressed women, and they look for the inner beauty.

> *If more girls would start respecting themselves*
> *guys would have no choice but to respect girls.*
> *You can't act like a rock*
> *and expect to be treated like a diamond.*
> —Unknown

How Do Women Dress Immodestly?

A concerned pastor, burdened by how some of the women of his church were dressing, prayerfully asked men to name immodest dressing. The pastor did not suggest that the women were intentionally dressing immodestly. Nor was he blaming the women for the men struggling with lust, since they needed to take responsibility for their sin. The pastor hoped that the men would honor their sisters in Christ since he knew that the way women often dressed was provocative. The men listed the ways that they found overtly sexual and distracting.

1. **Dresses or skirts with lengthy slits**
   When a man sees a long slit up a skirt or dress, he may think, "Oh, a few more inches and what would I see?" The slit is a magnet to men's eyes. That is the way a man's mind works.

   > *When a woman veils her body in modest clothing,*
   > *she is not hiding herself from men.*
   > *On the contrary, she is revealing her dignity to them.*
   > —Jason Evert

2. **Dresses, skirts (including tight pencil ones), shorts, or jeans that tightly cling to the backside and even down into the back of the thighs.**
   This does not mean *fitted* clothing but rather skintight apparel that draws men's attention.

   > *Modesty is not just covering up;*
   > *it is concealing body form.*

3. **A skintight top, blouse, or dress top.**
   Avoid skintight women's tops that reveal like an anatomy lesson identifying structural details to those who see them. Ask yourself, "Is this concealment? Is this dress dignified?" Instead, a woman's top should hang loosely.

   > *Choosing to dress modestly sends the message*
   > *that our face is where the focus needs to be.*
   > *Modesty encourages others to get*
   > *to know us, not our curves.*
   > —Unknown

4. **Unbuttoned blouses or dresses, low-neck lines, or cleavage.**

   A blouse that is unbuttoned too low may tempt a man's mind to wonder about things he should not. Women in church or other settings may need to bend over and pick up a child or other item. When standing up, you are sufficiently covered but not when you bend over. Women need to realize that when they bend forward the blouse or dress gaps away from the skin revealing what it should not. To avoid giving a free show place your hand on your blouse or dress top to hold it against your skin when you bend over. If the neckline is low, wear a dickey or an insert to cover yourself.

   > *What is the price of modesty?*
   > *You will not be a magnet for lustful people.*
   > *But you will probably attract someone*
   > *who knows the difference between love and lust.*
   >
   > —Unknown

5. **Sleeveless tops with large, gaping holes**

   A sleeveless dress or top with tight armholes is modest. But a large gaping armhole may cause a man behind you to see your undergarment and cause his mind to wander in the wrong direction.

6. **Low-rise skirts, shorts, or jeans**

   Avoid clothing that barely hangs on the hipbones or jeans/shorts that hang so low they reveal parts of the anatomy. Men should also consider modesty and avoid low-rise pants or shorts. Is this concealment? Is this dress dignified? If you do wear hip-hugger jeans/shorts, then modesty calls for an extra long top.

   > *Immodesty catches the eye.*
   > *Modesty draws the heart.*
   >
   > —Unknown

7. **Skirts, dresses, and shorts that are just too short**
   When a woman or girl has to pull down or shimmy to get her clothing to cover herself, the skirt, dress, or shorts are too short. Mini-skirts or micro-mini skirts lack enough material to *be* pulled down! Unfortunately, some girls and women aren't concerned and let their clothing rise where it may when she sits down. A good rule of thumb: wear these items just above the knee (Bermuda shorts style). When you try on clothes, sit and see if the item rides up, lean to the side and see if it goes high, bend forward and look at the back. A most attractive length for skirts and dresses is a hemline-hitting mid-knee or just under the knee. For many women, this hem length gives a balanced, proportionate look to a woman's figure.

   > *A man's eyes are drawn to where*
   > *the skin line and the clothing line meet.*
   > *If you do not want his eyes to go "there,"*
   > *don't put the skin clothing line there.*
   > —Unknown

8. **See-through clothing**
   A woman can be dressed head to toe and still be dressed immodestly. Immodesty can include transparent/revealing or tight-fitting clothes. Wear a slip or camisole under your clothing to conceal your underwear.

   > *Modestly dressing doesn't mean I lack confidence,*
   > *it means I'm so confident I don't need to reveal my body*
   > *to the world because I'd rather reveal my mind.*
   > —Unknown

9. **Skin-tight slacks, jeans, shorts, and leggings (like yoga pants) that tightly hug the backside, the thighs, or other private body areas.**
   Most girls and women have no idea how this type of clothing becomes a magnet for men's eyes where otherwise they may not

look. In addition to the backside and thighs, a woman's tight outline of other body parts will be a magnet for a guy's attention. Also, pink or skin colored clothing causes others to wonder. One man admitted that if guys were honest, they would tell you that this is every man's battle.

> *When a girl or woman dresses immodestly,*
> *she has no idea the battle a man goes thru*
> *to mentally focus or keep his thoughts pure.*
> *It's a mine field that he is trying to overcome.*
> *Ladies, don't be the battle for him to have to fight.*
> *Dress in honor for others and God.*
>
> —Jenny Williams,
> A Modern Day Ruth

In addition, men should also dress modestly and avoid tight clothing. Sadly, in our sexually degenerate culture, provocative attire may attract gay attentions as is common even among teens.

Be fashionable and modest by wearing an oversized, long shirt over leggings, one that covers the most of the thighs and other private areas. Layering is often a way to dress fashionably modest. For modesty and comfort, buy tops and pants in a size-up. Wear extra long T-shirts for active wear, Capris, and workout pants that fit loosely and avoid the clinging yoga or exercise pants or skin-tight Spandex, which reveals body shape.

Choose loose-fitting slacks, jeans, or shorts. Tight clothing makes us appear heavier. In addition, tight pants and shorts are linked to skin irritations and female infections. Modest shorts are knee length or a couple of inches above and conceal the private body parts.

> *When a woman veils her body in modesty,*
> *she is not hiding herself from men.*
> *She is revealing her dignity to them!*

Yes, it may be difficult to find modest clothing in retails stores. Searching for modest clothing online is another option. Shopping at resale or thrift shops will offer options such as cutting jeans into Bermuda length shorts or purchasing clothing a size-up, so it is not skin-tight. Use layering with clothes such as a long sweater or long vest. Be creative, pray for guidance, and remember you are dressing to honor your Savior.

10. A bare midriff and back

You may look in the mirror and think you're covered, but when you reach over a few inches, your tummy shows. If you bend over, you reveal your back and perhaps the top of the underwear or more.

> *Raise your hands and touch your toes,*
> *if anything shows, change your clothes.*
>
> —Unknown

11. Maternity attire

As we look at the 11th observation, maternity wear, remember that modesty originates in the heart and modesty is not just covering up; it is concealing body form. Keep the modesty principles in mind when you plan your maternity wardrobe.

Our culture has also forsaken modesty—decency and tastefulness—during pregnancy by encouraging women to be more revealing by showing more skin or wearing tighter clothing. Today, there is a desire for women to show off the baby bump. We honor the Lord by putting the spotlight on Him, not on ourselves.

> *Christians aren't called to draw attention to us;*
> *we are called to draw attention to Christ.*

Modest maternity clothes are tasteful, dignified, non-revealing but restrained (poised), and feminine. Maintaining dignity and honor as a representative of Christ is the believer's calling, whether pregnant or not. Therefore, you may have to be more creative in choosing attire that is modest and comfortable, as well as feminine and pretty. Pregnancy is a time for celebrating a new life but also a time to *point* others to Christ—not just an expanded midsection. Pray for God's guidance in planning a modest maternity wardrobe. He won't let you down!

> *Develop deep beauty.*
> *There is no more beautiful sight than a young woman*
> *who glows with the light of the Spirit,*
> *who is confident and courageous because she is virtuous.*
> *Mirror, Mirror on the wall, do I heed my Savior's call?*
> —Elaine Dalton

What Is Modest Attire for Other Situations?

Next, we examine swimwear and formal wear, since these were not on the churchmen's observation list.

Modest Swimwear

May a Christian woman ever wear immodest clothes that sexually arouse interest or desire? That depends upon the circumstances. Only a married woman could dress in a revealing way *but* only for her husband in a private setting.

In some public settings, may Christian women wear revealing clothing that exposes their private parts? Absolutely not! Women parading indecently in revealing and body conforming swimwear attract the wrong attention. Besides, what are we teaching little girls when we allow them to wear bikinis?

> *When it feels like the entire world is seducing you*
> *To wear miniskirts and bikinis just remember,*
> *godly guys find modesty attractive!*
> —Unknown

Current options for swimwear seem to lack a sense of attractiveness or decency. A Christian woman or girl will need to be creative by mixing-and-matching modest pieces. Perhaps you could pair a shirt with breathable fabric and longer-length shorts. An acceptable modest option is wearing a modest cover-up over your modest swimsuit when you are not in the water. Always ask, "What is honoring to God?"

Modesty isn't only about concealing your body form, it's about revealing your dignity.

Wedding Gowns, Prom Dresses, and Other Formal Attire

The same biblical principles of modesty apply formal attire such as wedding apparel, bridesmaid dresses, and prom dresses and the like.

Immodesty is conforming and revealing.
Modesty is tasteful, dignified, non-suggestive.

Don't give in and compromise your standards when searching for formal attire. Instead, give in to Christ, pray for a modest gown, and trust Him to provide. Your godly choice will honor the Lord and may bless others as well.

Are People Offended by Today's Immodesty?

Modesty is rarely seen in this generation of Christians.
Many who claim Christ are as uncovered, lewd and brazen as the world.

—Paul Washer

You may be surprised to know that girls and women who dress immodestly (indecently) are often wearing the attire of a harlot. What harlots wore years ago has now become the fashion, even among many Christian women. Today's women dress immodestly with no shame. Preteen and teen girls, women (married or unmarried), pregnant women, middle-aged women—and, yes, even women of grandmother age—have yielded to provocative dress trends. Either they dress that way because of ignorance, or they have been charmed by Satan's deceits.

How distressing that so many Christian women have strayed from modest dress (as have men). Now they embrace the world's (Satan's) indecent fashions that trigger lustful thoughts. What ought to evoke shame and displeasure are what give some women happiness. Many Christian women have become so accustomed to seeing provocative attire that now they embrace it. They have become desensitized to the new normal. Notice the downward spiral of a compromising believer starts with *recognizing error* then *tolerates error,* next *excuses error,* then *defends error,* then *condones error,* then *embraces error.*

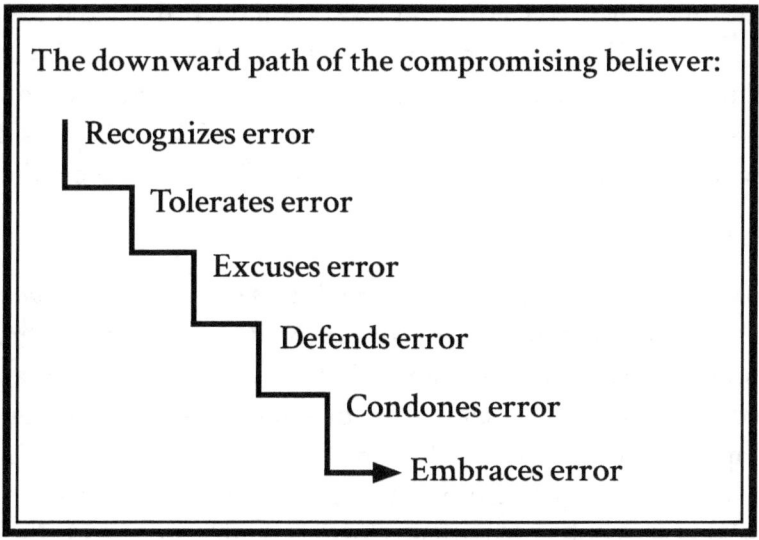

The downward path of the compromising believer:
- Recognizes error
- Tolerates error
- Excuses error
- Defends error
- Condones error
- Embraces error

*What one generation tolerates,
the next generation will embrace.*
—John Wesley

We know that sin contaminates so we must raise walls of separation. When we mingle with the world, we often slide down the compromising path; just one compromise will lead to another. When we fail to pass down God's values on modesty to the next generation, we enable the world to defile them. By keeping silent, we allow others to compromise in one area of Christian living, and more compromising will follow. We are losing the next generation by our compromise, our complacency, and our silence

> *Our world desperately needs to see*
> *Christian girls and women*
> *who have the courage and are willing*
> *to say NO to compromise and YES to the Lord.*
>
> —Unknown

Many husbands and fathers are unwilling to say something to their wives or daughters about modesty. Conversely, many men do lead in their homes, express their concerns, and insist on modest dress and conduct. However, many Christian women won't submit to their husband's authority, and the daughters may follow their mother's examples. Also, contrary to God's command to admonition one another (Col. 3:16; Titus 2:3-5; Romans 15:14), many Christian women hesitate to confront another.

How should we confront someone who dresses or behaves immodestly? Just as Jesus confronted the woman caught in the act of adultery, we also should confront in love (John 8). When we see someone wearing a spaghetti-strap top, a very short skirt, or some skin-tight clothing, wait for an appropriate time to speak with her. If she isn't saved by faith in Christ, share the gospel before confronting. When confronting, speak the truth in love (Eph. 4:15)—that is love through actions and His truth. We remember that we are also sinners and pray that you do not appear judgmental or self-righteous. Asking a question is often a good opening. Pray for the right words to inform her of the facts of immodesty and pray that she would be receptive to your words.

> *Let us not love with words or speech*
> *but with actions and in truth.*
>
> —1 John 3:18

Concluding considerations. We have examined five principles on modesty, which are not optional; they are God's mandates. Modesty is primarily a matter of the heart. As living temples of the Holy Spirit, we respect our temple with modest dress. As His temple, I need to consider, "do my clothing choices *reflect* what I *believe* then what *beliefs* do my clothing choices *reflect*?" By demonstrating *agape* love with modest appearance, we avoid causing another to be distracted or tempted to sin. Lights of Christ in a fallen, dark world won't be conformed to and blend in with the world. As lights we keep separate (set apart) from the world's standards. Finally, by choosing to follow God's principles of modesty, we present a spiritual, living sacrifice to God—a pleasing spiritual act of worship.

A godly woman with true beauty draws attention to Christ.
She is a woman with a heart to be separate
from the world in all her ways.
Her appearance, her words, and her actions
reflect her love for Jesus Christ, her Savior.

Study Questions

Cite Scripture verses when possible.

1. What is modesty?

2. How can immodest dressing cause offense to another believer?

3. How can provocative dress cause another to sin?

4. Name five biblical principles why you should dress modestly.

5. How will you apply this information to your life?

CHAPTER 12

What You Need to Know to Avoid Sexual Temptation

*Did you ever wonder why God gave us a sex drive
and then tells us to wait?
Have Satan's lies regarding sex deceived you?
Are you interested in God's foolproof strategies
to avoid sinful entrapment?*

This chapter will:

- ♥ Provide biblical answers to those questions.

- ♥ Disclose other dating dangers.

- ♥ Supply scriptural tactics for victory over temptation.

God designed us with longings and needs so we would depend on Him to fulfill them in His timing. Satan's purpose is distorting our craving for love into lust, our yearning for respect into pride, and our hope for achievement into greed. Distorted desires can become destructive behaviors. In the same way, God gave us the need to eat food; however, we can harm our bodies by misusing this need by overeating, by consuming risky foods or drinks, or by starving ourselves to stay thin. Satan always has a substitute offer for God's best. God doesn't disapprove of natural needs such as food, achievement, or love, but He opposes overindulgence, especially outside His lovingly designed limits. Of the gifts God gave to people, sex is the most abused and is Satan's grand deception.

Satan is no fool; his timing is good;
he waits until you are in deep trouble,
and then he lets you have it.

—Dale Evans Rogers

Why Does God Give Sexual Desire and Then Say "Wait"?

Randy and Liza walked into the pastor's office, and during the conversation asked, "Why does God give us intense sexual desire if He didn't want us to fulfill it?" This argument seems convincing and logical to some who rationalize, "What kind of God gives His creatures sexual cravings but then commands they shouldn't fulfill them? But the right question is: "How does God want me to fulfill my sexual desires?"

Another couple taking premarital counseling confessed to the pastor that they had been sleeping together. They defended their actions by explaining their strong attraction to each other and added, "God understands because He allows us to feel this way." The pastor looked the man straight in the eye and asked, "What would you do if you met a woman at work and you feel strong physical attraction? Would you use the same justification: If God didn't want me to meet this need, He wouldn't let me feel this way." Although our Creator God created us with specific yearnings, our sin nature wants to manipulate and misdirect those desires.

The more fully the Lord Jesus controls within,
the less we will be influenced by externals.
The more we are affected by externals,
the less freedom He will have within.

—None But the Hungry Heart, 3-13

Why Are Sexual Sins Increasing?

Why are growing numbers of Christians, even pastors, yielding to sexual immorality? As Christians, we stand for biblical marriage between one man and one woman, so why are we witnessing this increasing wave of sexual moral failure?

We could blame simple access to pornography, sex-saturated films, music, games, commercials, or Satan and his demons. Although sexually saturated forms of entertainment influence us, and pressure us to tolerate and then embrace such behaviors, they don't force us to sin. Sin is a choice to enjoy its pleasures. The Bible tells us who is to blame. The responsibility lies in the human heart (Jeremiah 17:9). *"For out of the heart come evil thoughts, murder, adultery, sexual immorality, theft, false testimony, slander"* (Matthew 15:19 NIV). Contrary to public opinion, no one nor the Devil *makes* us sin.

The soil of our heart affects the fruit
of our lips and actions.

The Sin of Pride Underlies All Sin

The sin of pride is a form of self-love and self-righteousness. Pride exaggerates our view of ourselves. However, God wants us to see the truth about ourselves—that we fall short of God's standards (Romans 3:23). Recognizing that no one measures up, all are sinful, and all are guilty should humble us. Pride rejects the authority of God's Word, will, and plan.

How Does Pride Apply to Dating?
Pride is yet another danger of dating that stunts spiritual growth. For example:

- √ Because they want attention from men, women may entice men.

- √ A woman may flirt or entice a guy because another girl is interested in him.

- √ Some prideful women gain self-worth from attractiveness, from popularity, or from the fashions they wear.

- √ An exaggerated opinion of himself— "thinks *he's* great," because he's consumed with himself (also applies to the woman).

- √ When one woman told a man that she wants a man to love the Lord more than her, he became upset.

- √ A man may see himself as having authority, so he takes advantage of a woman, which hurts her.

How Is Rebellion a Dating Danger?

The pride of having your way is rebellion. People sin when they rebel against God by rejecting His standards. When people don't align themselves with God's principles, their relationship with their Father collapses. *"The fear of the LORD is the beginning of knowledge, But fools despise wisdom and instruction"* (Proverbs 1:7). By refusing to obey Father God in the dating process, they reject His will, which is rebellion.

Contrary to God's will and timing,
Satan wants us to fulfill God-given desires
hastily and easily.

The Struggles of a Slave to Sexual Sin

Notice the sins of pride, rebellion, idolatry in this next example.

> Max, a young Christian friend, confided that he became a slave to sexual sin with his former girlfriend. He could think of nothing except his next sexual encounter. As Max shared with me his struggles, it saddened me to see him distraught. Max revealed that he became overwhelmed with guilt that led to depression. Eventually, he confessed his sins, believed the Lord forgave him (1 John 1:9), and prayed for God's help to overcome promiscuity. For over a year Max prayed for freedom from sexual bondage. Max repeatedly said how good God was to him to deliver him from this sin. The effects of this particular sin were so devastating that he warns others: "Don't even think you can get away with it." *"For God will bring every act to judgment, everything which is hidden, whether it is good or evil"* (Ecclesiastes 12:14).

> *Hidden sin is an open scandal in heaven.*

> I hate sin when I see what it does to human beings. I hate sin most when I see what it did to Christ! It turned the fairest face that ever was into a bruised and bloody thing [as part of God's punishment for sin]. When sin did that to the Son of God, how can you ever play with it again?
> —Ian MacPherson

Question: How can we break the obsession with sexual sin?
In a pastor's office, a young woman expressed her concern. "Although my boyfriend and I are Christians, we are sexually active. We know we are sinning because God tells us to wait until we are married. But no matter how hard we try to abstain, we yield to sexual temptation. We live four hours apart so see each other once a week, but despite our good

intentions to abstain, we fall into our old behavior. How can we break the cycle and get right with God?"

Answer:
To break the obsession with sexual sin, you need to *change your habits and your thinking*. You need to breakup or stop spending time alone. The second half of victory over temptation depends on your *believing God's truths*.

You may repeatedly try without success to stop sinning. Paul faced challenges of the *power* of sin and lamented, *"What a wretched man I am! Who will rescue me from this body of death?"* (Romans 7:24 NIV).

Warren Wiersbe explains,

> Romans 7:21-25 does not suggest that you live a divided life because that is impossible. You must choose your master (6:15-23) and be true to your Husband, Jesus Christ (7:1-6). "The mind" refers to the new nature from God and "the body of death" the old nature from Adam. We cannot serve God with an old nature that is sinful (7:18), but the Holy Spirit enables us to do His will as we yield to Him. The human body is not sinful, but the human nature is.

God's Rescue Plan over the *Power* of Sin

God has provided a rescue plan from temptation and the *power* of sin. Because we are united in Christ, we have the benefit of trusting in God and not ourselves to deliver us from the power of sin. *"Knowing this, that our old man was crucified with Him, that the body of sin might be done away with, that we should no longer be slaves of sin.' For he who has died has been freed from sin"* (Romans 6:6-7).

> The death of the Lord Jesus was not only an atonement for sins, but a triumph over sin. By faith we see our sins not only

> on His head for our pardon, but sin under His feet for our deliverance. Multitudes who glory in the outward Cross no nothing of that inward crucifixion which it has also made possible, whereby they are delivered from the power of self and sin, the world, the flesh, and the devil. That they do not know: That their 'old man was crucified with him, that the body of sin might be done away, so that they should no longer live in bondage to sin' (Romans 6:6).
>
> —G. Marshall, quoted by Miles Stanford,
> *None But the Hungry Heart*, 8-11.

The "old man" refers to everything we were in Adam—the original spiritual family into which we were born. In Adam's family, we were God's enemy, we hated God, and we were in opposition to God. We were deceived followers of Satan and slaves to sin because sin dominated or ruled our life.

> We are not only to take by faith the fact that the Lord Jesus died for us to pay the price and penalty for our sins, but we are to appropriated by faith the fact that He also took us to the Cross with Him. In Christ God put to death our old man that we might be delivered from the power and domination of sin in our lives. So the story of the pathway of faith begins with Calvary and our identification with the crucifixion of the Lord Jesus.
>
> —G. Marshall, quoted in Miles Stanford,
> *None But the Hungry Heart*, 8-11

As believers, we are dead to the old life in Adam (dead to sin), but alive in Christ to God.

> The most vivid illustration of Romans six is Lazarus (John 11). Jesus raised him from the dead and then said, "loose him, and let him go" (John 11:44). Lazarus left the grave, got rid of the grave clothes, and became a new life (Col. 3:1ff.). God's

people are both "dead" and "alive" (Romans 6:11), and by faith must live accordingly.

—Warren Wiersbe

Christ's death not only satisfied the *penalty* (punishment) for our sin but He also died to the *power* of sin. Since we were spiritually crucified with Him (Romans 6:6) and were united in His death, God freed us from both the *penalty* and the *power* of sin. Because we died spiritually with Christ, we are *dead* to sin. Since "death" means separation, this *death* to sin *separates or frees* us from sin's control or authority in our life. Therefore, when we're tempted, we should recall that we can *choose not* to respond. By faith we choose to depend on the Spirit's enablement, not ourselves, so the Lord gets the glory.

When a Christian considers the truths of Romans 6:11, the Spirit of God enables him to say "no" to temptation. *"Likewise you also, reckon yourselves to be dead indeed to sin, but alive to God in Christ Jesus our Lord." Therefore do not let sin reign* [rule] *in your mortal body, that you should obey it in its lusts"* (Romans 6:11-12). When Christians live from their position in Christ under the control of the Spirit of God, it is possible to say no to sexual immorality.

A lack of trust in God's provisions opens the door to sin.

Claiming the Victory You Already Have!

By your faith in Christ's finished cross work, you can realize the victory over the *power* of sin is complete—you already have victory in Christ.

> The believer is never told to *'overcome sin,'* but to reckon, on the ground of his death with Christ, that he has died to it. On the basis of death, he is told not to 'let' sin reign in his life. It is to be dealt with by an attitude of death, not by 'overcoming.' The believer therefore is *not* to be spending his whole life

in getting victory over sin, but understanding his position as having died unto sin.

—Miles Stanford,
None But The Hungry Heart, 4-31.

Paul states in Romans 8 that when we stop struggling not to sin and rely on the Holy Spirit, He delivers us in daily life from sin's rule.

> Victory comes through the reckoning of faith and not through struggling and striving. 'But,' it may be asked, 'are we not exhorted to 'fight the good fight'? Yes, that is so, but you must please finish the text, 'Fight the good fight of faith,' and faith never struggles for victory. Faith stands in victory.
>
>
>
> —Miles Stanford,
> *None But The Hungry Heart*, 2-22
>
>

1. **We don't fight *for* victory; we fight *from* victory.**
   Do you swallow the bait of enticement? When temptation confronts you with a lustful glance, an X-rated movie or website, or a shameless sexual advance, do you have an exit plan (biblical thoughts and escape routes) prepared? When faced with temptation, do we play with it, talk to it, stroke it, analyze it, revisit it, or do we run away?

   > *Better to shun the bait than struggle in the snare.*
   >
   > —John Dryden

2. **Use Scripture as a weapon of escape.**
   The power of the Spirit alone can enable you to prevail against the sins of sexual immorality. The Word of God circulating in your mind is the Spirit's weapon for victory over temptation. *"No temptation has overtaken you except such as is common to man; but God is faithful, who will not allow you to be tempted beyond what you are able, but with the temptation will also make the way of escape, that you may be able to bear it"* (1 Corinthians 10:13).

An excellent devotional titled "God Is So Faithful" explains this verse in detail.
Listen at http://www.wogbc.org/messages/?sermon_id=931

When Jesus was tempted,
He always quoted Scripture as His defense (Luke 4:1-13).

Just as we can't flee a burning building if we don't know where the exits are, we can't escape temptation without knowing the escape route. Our exit plan from temptation includes reflecting on or quoting Scripture. When tempted by Potiphar's wife, the biblical Joseph used a verbal statement and then fled the house. *"How then can I do this great wickedness, and sin against God?"* (Genesis 39:9b). Another exit verse is *"Therefore submit to God. Resist the devil and he will flee from you"* (James 4:7).

When you flee from temptation, do not leave a
forwarding address behind.

3. **Be alert and pray.**
   When temptations come, call upon Him in prayer to avoid falling into temptation. As Christ commanded His disciples, *"Watch and pray so that you will not fall into temptation. The spirit is willing, but the body is weak"* (Matthew 26:41 NIV). Since your position is in Christ and He indwells you, you are always together. Wherever you go, your Savior is with you (Matthew 28:20).

4. **Follow God's principle of purity.**
   You recall that we live the Christian life first in our thinking, followed by feelings, behaviors, and actions. Therefore, victory comes through occupation with Christ and His Word, including His prevention principles to avoid temptation or sexual impurity. The following are some of God's protection principles.

My son, keep your father's commands and do not forsake your mother's teaching.

²¹ Bind them upon your heart forever; fasten them around your neck.
²² When you walk, they will guide you; when you sleep, they will watch over you; when you awake, they will speak to you.
²³ For these commands are a lamp, this teaching is a light, and the corrections of discipline are the way to life,
²⁴ keeping you from the immoral woman, from the smooth tongue of the wayward wife.
²⁵ Do not lust in your heart after her beauty or let her captivate you with her eyes,
²⁶ for the prostitute reduces you to a loaf of bread, and the adulteress preys upon your very life.
²⁷ Can a man scoop fire into his lap without his clothes being burned?
²⁸ Can a man walk on hot coals without his feet being scorched?
²⁹ So is he who sleeps with another man's wife; no one who touches her will go unpunished (Proverbs 6:20-29 NIV).

> *Sin is not hurtful because it is forbidden,*
> *but it is forbidden because it is hurtful.*
> —Benjamin Franklin

In summary, Christians are a new creation in Christ, but we still have a sin nature. We live in a sinful world where the Devil and the world around us tempt us. When we recognize the weakness of our flesh (sin nature) and set clear boundaries, we prevent opportunities for the flesh, the self-will, to sin. God always provides a way of escape from sin's enticement or entrapments. We can quote Scripture and recall God's principles as part of our exit or escape plan. Our choice is either follow our sin nature or live from our position in Christ. By faith, we consider ourselves dead to sin; thus, we have victory over temptation. Jesus commanded His disciples to pray to avoid giving into temptation (Matthew 26:41). Prayer is the remedy to escape falling into temptation.

> *True freedom is not having our own way*
> *but yielding to God's way.*
> —CBZ

Study Questions

Please provide Scripture proofs to your answers when possible.

1. Why does God give us a sex drive and then tell us to wait?

2. The failure to understand the truths of Scripture, especially their _____ in Christ, is the primary reason for sin among believers.

3. To what does the "old man" refer?

4. As believers in Christ we are _____ to the old life in _____ but _____ in Christ to _____. Cite scripture verse for this statement.

5. Why can't we stop sinning just by trying hard?

6. Christ's death not only satisfied the *penalty* (punishment) of our sin but He also died to the _____ of sin. Since we were spiritually _____ with Him (Romans 6:6), and were _____ in His death, we are freed from both the *penalty* and the *power* of sin.

7. Dead to sin means _____ from the authority or _____ of sin.

8. How can the truth that you are spiritually dead to sin influence your life?

9. Explain "you already have victory in Christ."

10. Since your flesh is powerless to stop sinning, who enables you to claim your continuing victory in Christ? How does this happen?

11. Explain three scriptural strategies to avoid yielding to sin's entrapment.

12. Because we are united in Christ we have the advantage of _____ in God and not ourselves, to _____ us from the *power* of sin.

CHAPTER 13

What You Need to Know about Bonding

**Have you set boundaries for protecting your purity?
What do abstinence, boundaries, and bonding have in common?**

In this chapter you will:

- ♥ Learn the benefits of practicing abstinence as a single person by understanding the 12 stages of sexual intimacy.

- ♥ Discover how abstinence and setting physical boundaries improve bonding and contribute to a contented marriage.

- ♥ Observe how God protects single people from harmful results when they live according to His plan by waiting until marriage.

- ♥ Read about seven recommendations for a satisfied marriage.

Numerous individuals have no clue about setting boundaries to avoid premarital sex. If you are unaware of the steps towards sexual intimacy and fail to draw proper limits, you will easily yield to temptation.

Satan's Undermining of God's Marriage Blueprint Persists

Since society overturned standards governing sexual conduct, our culture is reaping severe consequences. Now with over 70 years of lower standards, we live with an epidemic of more than 20 sexually transmitted diseases (STDs), with devastating new microbes appearing every few years. In addition to STDs, resulting cancers and AIDS cause suffering to individuals for a lifetime. Promiscuity results in millions of men and women having babies out of wedlock or having abortions. Probably the most devastating consequence is the damage to the family institution.

Even non-Christians think the sexual revolution was a disaster. They agree with Christians that abstinence before marriage and lifelong faithfulness are best for individuals and society. Some sociologists have also rediscovered the benefits of sexual restraint—as the Bible maintained for thousands of years. However, those unwilling to accept the moral values of Scripture continue to search for ways to promote promiscuity without the risks. By promoting safe sex through condom use, they pretend they are protecting people from dangerous diseases. But when an individual chooses to behave in direct contradiction to God's laws, no one can hide from consequences. Sin always causes damages. The Bible alone has provided a safe place for safe sex—it's called marriage!

Rejecting God's way is simply asking for trouble.
—CBZ

What Does the Bible Mean by Sexual Immorality?

Galatians 5:19 lists four immoral acts: adultery, fornication, uncleanness, and lewdness. The Scriptures state that fornication includes every unlawful sexual relation: pre-marital sex (1Corinthians 7:1-2); adultery (Matthew 19:9); homosexuality/lesbianism (Romans 1:26-28); prostitution (1 Timothy 1:9-10); incest (1 Corinthians 5:1); and bestiality (Leviticus 20:15-16). Immoral behaviors are serious problems among

Christian teens and adults. Also, the increasing permissiveness of our culture has infiltrated the church for decades.

People understand that "fornication" is illicit sex between unmarried individuals, but it includes more. The Merriam-Webster dictionary defines the term "sexual intercourse" as "physical, sexual contact between an individual that involves the genitalia of a least one person." This definition further explains that this conduct is not limited to the sex act, but includes other contacts (touching—petting, making out) of sexual body parts. Therefore, fornication is *any* sexual contact between two people not married to each other.

The strong, God-given sexual longing isn't sinful, but with it comes the responsibility to maintain control over it, to set boundaries for physical contact, and wait for marriage.

Ask not, How far can I go,
but how close can I stay to my Savior?

The following list answers that question. Although the description of the 12 stages of physical and sexual intimacy has been available for years, many haven't seen it. As you read the list, keep in mind that sexual abstinence is essential before marriage and consider how purity correlates to bonding.

The 12 Stages of Sexual Intimacy

The first eight stages correspond to bonding, and therefore the sequence is important. However, the last four stages (reserved for marriage only) have no sequence priority.

Eye to Body
A glance at someone reveals much about that person—gender, size, age, perhaps even clues about personality and status.

Eye to Eye

The exchange of a glance may start a friendship. However, when a man and a woman exchange glances, their natural reaction is to look away, which may suggest uneasiness. But if their eyes meet again, they may smile, signaling the wish to become better acquainted.

Voice to Voice

Early conversations comprise trivia such as name exchanges, what employment you have, hobbies or pastimes, and likes and dislikes. Next is sharing opinions, dreams and goals, and other details of life. If they seem compatible, they become friends. Conversations may lead to bonding and help them determine whether that person is a possible lifetime mate.

The voice-to-voice stage of communication is important before you start a physical bond. A physical bond too early can push the emotional and intellectual aside. This could result in sharing personal information too soon with the wrong person.

Hand to Hand

At first physical contact between couples is non-romantic such as when a man helps the woman across the street or helps her out of the car. Since these are noncommittal actions, they offer a person the choice to refrain from a relationship. However, hand-to-hand contact could initiate holding hands, which would show evidence of a couple's romantic attachment to each other. At this stage keep on talking and enjoying each other's company.

Hand to Shoulder

This buddy position of the man and a woman side-by-side facing forward may be a fond cuddle but is noncommittal. At this stage, the communication is going well. Each person finds the other interesting and fun. This contact reveals a relationship more than friendship but probably not genuine love.

Hand to Waist

This physical touch makes a statement about your bonding and suggests you enjoy each other and have become familiar with personality and preferences. The couple walking side-by-side is close enough to share personal conversation, and yet they are still facing forward.

Face to Face

This stage of contact involves looking into each other's eyes and includes hugging and kissing. By following the previous steps sequentially, the couple will have developed a deep rapport that enables them to communicate with few words. At this bonding point, sexual desire becomes central.

> *Caution:* One kiss may easily lead to excessive kissing with the temptation to continue moving through the steps. Therefore, since a kiss is intimate, sensible individuals would benefit from choosing to save the first kiss for the wedding night—keeping it private and special for your spouse. You won't be sorry!

Hand to Head

This contact is an extension of the previous stage. In this stage, the man and woman cradle or caress each other's head while talking. In our culture, touching someone's head is rare, except those with whom we are romantically involved or a family member. Touching the head suggests emotional closeness—familiarity and comfort.

> *Caution:* An earlier chapter stated that when couples feel infatuation or love, the love hormones PEA, dopamine, and norepinephrine increase—as does testosterone (since lust is involved). Also, keep in mind the good feeling hormone oxytocin increases with physical touching.

The Final Steps

Although these are numbered, these last four steps of involvement are not necessarily progressive. They are (9) Hand to Body, (10) Mouth to Breast, (11) Touching below the waist and (12) Intercourse.

God reserved these final stages of intimate contact for marriage since they are increasingly sexual and intensely private. Statistics reveal that skipping this bonding progression while dating increases the risk of divorce.

If you have sex before you marry, you are also more likely to

- √ Breakup before you marry.

- √ Scare off someone who wants to marry a virgin.

- √ Feel less contented in your marriage.

- √ Get a divorce.

- √ Commit adultery after you marry.

- √ Marry for the wrong reason.

- √ Feel dissatisfaction with your marital sex life.

- √ Suffer guilt and rush into a poor marriage.

- √ Feel deprived of the important bonding that sexual intimacy can give a marriage.

*Source: Ray E. Short. *Sex, Dating, and Love*, 1994 Augsburg Publishing House.

The Progression of the Bonding Stage

For a male-female relationship to achieve its full potential, physical intimacy must continue slowly. When a man and woman deeply love each other and commit for life, they develop a record of understanding between them that others might consider insignificant. The couple shares numerous memories unique to their relationship. Their sense of specialness for each other originates from those private memories.

Taking the physical bonding steps in sequence is a significant reason for their strong association. When a couple reaches the later stages prematurely (such as when a couple kisses passionately or has premarital sex), they lose something precious from the relationship. Instead, nurture dating through leisurely walks, long talks, and lovers' secrets, which establish the basis for mutual intimacy. If a couple doesn't achieve mutual intimacy, the relationship remains shallow.

Mutual intimacy could include agreeing, adjusting, or compromising your thinking on issues. Topics to discuss include:

1. How many children do you want?

2. Where will you reside?

3. Would you be able to accept a long-distance marriage because of employment?

4. Will the wife work outside the home?

5. If the breadwinner loses his job, will he find part-time work while looking for work? If feasible, will the wife work to supplement? Will both work until the husband finds full-time work?

6. Will the husband support his wife and help with housework if the wife needs to work to help support the family?

7. To what extent will the husband help around the house?

8. How much will the husband-father involve himself with the children?

9. How will you spend the holidays—with her family or with yours?

10. Whose church will become our church?

11. How will you encourage the spiritual, emotional, and intellectual growth of your spouse?

12. When interests and preferences of your spouse don't interest you, how will you respond?

13. Are you able to accept personal dreams and goals that are different from your own?

Our culture of sexual permissiveness and lust contributes to the weakening of marriage and *undermines* the stability of the family. The emotional and spiritual bonding of two people must come before physical involvement. Marriages primarily based on physical/sexual involvements are more likely to fail than those based on knowing one another, sharing a common faith and values, and building memories. Emotional bonding links a man and a woman together, causing them to be deeply valuable to each other. That special bonding sets a couple apart from others and is God's gift of marital companionship for a man and a woman.

> *Physical intimacy or romantic love*
> *isn't what keep couples together.*
> *Instead, the spiritual and emotional traits*
> *make marriage engaging and appealing.*

While you are dating, keep in mind God's principles that will shape a possible future marriage. The following recommendations are summary points.

Seven Recommendations for a Successful Marriage

1. When you feel you have found the right person, don't rush the dating phase. Bonding takes about a year, and for some couples, it may take longer.

2. Carefully pray about choosing your marital partner; avoid impulsive or reckless decisions. Think long and seriously about the will of God in the matter. Keep relying on the Lord to guide you in the most important decision of your life. If you wait for the Lord, He will guide you.

3. Practice displaying *agape* love in your Christian life and let it overflow into dating.

4. Respect for a husband will make him want to love his wife more.

5. As you date for mate selection, continue through the *early* stages of intimacy in sequence. Keep talking and getting to know each other.

6. Virginity is one of the best foundations for a healthy marriage. Individuals who have reserved themselves only for a spouse's pleasure and love bring added meaning to the marriage bed. Besides, by following God's plan to wait until marriage, you protect the reproductive system from diseases often contracted through immoral sex. Understand that when you are sexually intimate with a promiscuous person, you are engaging in sex with every person whom that individual has had relations within the past ten years! Also, promiscuity places emotional burdens on individuals. Therefore, guarding your virginity

before marriage not only keeps you from sin but is also a healthy approach.

However, if you do find a nonvirgin whom you'd like to marry, you'll need to discern whether you can live with this knowledge. If past promiscuity is something you cannot accept or forgive, then end the relationship. Terminating a relationship now is better than harming a marriage. The ultimate question is, "Can I trust the person I'm dating?"

7. The dating couple should use the 12 stages list to set boundaries of physical intimacy that would please the Lord. While some people say stages one through eight are appropriate, others would recommend a boundary of one through six. As the potential spiritual leader, a wise man would take the lead in setting firm boundaries that honor the Lord.

Stages 9–12 are reserved exclusively for marriage, so guard your purity. If, however, you have lost your virginity, choose now to practice abstinence (secondary virginity) without wavering.

The stops of a good man are ordered of the Lord as well as the steps.

—CBZ

Study Questions

When possible, provide Scripture proofs to your answers.

1. Give specifics on how abstinence, boundaries, and bonding benefit marriage.

2. Why is the progression through the bonding process essential to a strong relationship?

3. How do abstinence and setting boundaries improve bonding and contribute to a contented marriage?

4. Statistics reveal that skipping the bonding progression increases the risk of _____ _____.

5. Why is mutual intimacy so important?

6. What important facts will you take with you from this chapter?

CHAPTER 14

Happily Single— How to Have Ultimate Peace

Are your concerns about finding someone to marry
consuming your thoughts?
Does God have the perfect spouse for you?
Do you have anxiety about your future if you remain single?
Do you believe God is sovereign over everything?

In this chapter you will discover:

- ♥ The principles of God's peace.

- ♥ How to rely on God's sovereignty.

- ♥ How to stop worrying whether you remain single or marry.

- ♥ That waiting on the Lord isn't the same as inactivity.

Will You Trust God, the Perfect Matchmaker?
Excerpt from LifeQuakes—God's Rescue Plan in Hard Times

Each situation for selecting a mate is unique. Some court, some prefer random dating, and others participate in principled dating. Still, others may notice a possible mate and get to know them without dating. Notice the manner in which the next couple became acquainted and eventually married.

Dan writes,

> At age 30 and on my way to the mission field in Albania, I had resolved that I probably would never marry. Since I had made wrong selections in the past, I had no desire to date ever again. I felt if the Lord wanted me to marry, He would make it happen. Since God's ways are higher than our ways, I left the matter in His capable hands.
>
> As I did ministry, God positioned a believer named Bruni as my interpreter. As time passed, I began to wonder if the Lord wanted Bruni and me to marry. When I returned to the U.S., I began praying that Bruni and I know the Lord's will for us. We stayed in contact through email. When I returned to Albania, I expressed my feelings for her and we agreed to pray for the Lord's reassurance about His will. We did missionary work together but never once dated, and we remained pure during this time. *"Flee sexual immorality. Every sin that a man does is outside the body, but he who commits sexual immorality sins against his own body"* (1 Corinthians 6:18). We didn't want anything to hinder us from knowing the Lord's will.
>
> After six months, the Lord convinced us that His will for us was marriage. Even during our engagement, we decided to limit physical contact so our dating and marriage would honor the Lord. *"Your word I have hidden in my heart, That I might not sin against You!"* (Psalm 119:11). We decided only to hold hands during our engagement. This idea of limited physical contact sounds ridiculous by today's immoral standards, but this was our conviction. After our two-month engagement, we married and had our first kiss during our wedding ceremony. We had our first child, Esther, about nine months and one week later.
>
> The Lord directed my path as He promised He would if I trusted Him (Proverbs 3:5-6). When I look back at how

our relationship began, I have no regrets. I thank the Lord Jesus Christ for my wife, Bruni, and our four children. I have learned it's always best to wait for God's plan and timing.

Our Sovereign God always gives His best to those who leave the choice to Him.

Does God Have the Perfect Spouse for You?

Nowhere in Scripture does God suggest a perfect person for you to marry. Nor does He command you to marry a specific person. God loves you and gives you a choice whether to marry and a choice of whom to marry. But God does have a clear command about whom we choose to marry; He commands us not to marry an unsaved person. *"Do not be mismatched with unbelievers. For what partnership is there between righteousness and lawlessness? Or what fellowship is there between light and darkness? 15 What agreement does Christ have with Belial? Or what does a believer share with an unbeliever?"* (2 Corinthians 6:14-15 NRSV). A Christian may choose whom to marry as long as the prospect is saved (1 Corinthians 7:39), but ultimately choosing a spouse calls for God's grace, wisdom, prayer, and godly counsel.

God's Word states that He is interested in how you treat the one you marry (Ephesians 5:22-33). A principle to remember: When you are walking in the Spirit (relying on God), He honors choices that reflect His will or guidance. Therefore, He will recognize your choice and bless you according to His will.

Believing a perfect spouse exists, leads to unrealistic expectations in a marriage. Several individuals might be a suitable spouse for you. Don't let someone push you towards marriage or convince you that this person is the one. You may have doubts about the selection others think is the person for you. Even though your family member or a close friend may influence you, the prayerful consideration of a possible mate is between you and the Lord.

Karen discloses,

> I knew the choice to marry Peter was mine before the Lord right up to the moment I took the marriage vows. My belief that there is no perfect mate since all are sinners was helpful to me. When I had doubts, this conviction made me less vulnerable to what others told me, "This is God's will for you" and "This is God's perfect choice for you."

However, when believers are yielding to the Spirit of God for guidance and direction in their lives, He always does what is best for them. When a believer seeks the Lord for a spouse, the Lord will work behind the scenes to provide the best suitable mate in His perfect timing. If marriage is not in His plan for your life, He will guide and comfort you in other ways. God's plan for your life is tailor-made and expresses the love He has for you (Jeremiah 29:11).

> *When choosing whom to date*
> *and whom to select for a spouse,*
> *biblical discernment is essential.*

Are You Worried about Your Future?

Do you envy others because they are married? Do you sense that God has let you down and has neglected to provide you with a mate? Are you worried about growing old alone?

Take time now to complete this self-evaluation inventory by truthfully answering questions and skipping those that don't apply.

1. Has finding a mate become a priority instead of trusting the Lord to provide?

2. Do I believe God is in control of my life including my singleness?

3. Am I "casting all [my] care upon Him, for He cares for [me]" (1 Peter 5:7)?

4. Do I trust that nothing is too difficult for the Lord?

5. Do I believe the Lord can do whatever He chooses? If so, will I surrender my needs, problems, circumstances—even my life—to His supreme management?

6. Is the Lord the supreme manager of my finances?

7. Have I entrusted my health concerns to the Lord who perfectly manages health care?

8. Do I believe the Lord knows best in every circumstance whether He changes something or not?

9. Have I given my difficulties with people to Him who knows everything?

> *Those who see God's hand in everything*
> *can best leave everything in God's hand.*
>
> —CBZ

Accepting God's Sovereignty

Your relationship with Christ determines your capacity for accepting God's plan for your life. Because Ruth chose to obey God's command not to marry an unsaved person, she declined a marriage proposal from the man she loved. Her desire to follow God's plan and receive His blessings superseded having her way. Ruth understood that trusting and obeying

God were the way to have joy in the Lord. In lifelong singleness, she continued to have confidence in God's wisdom for her life. The sufficiency of Christ, her spiritual Bridegroom, fulfilled her.

> When once we see and accept our Father's purpose for our lives to the extent that it becomes our will also, the time and details of His process cease to matter. "Thy will be done" (Luke 11:2).
>
> —Miles Stanford,
> *None But the Hungry Heart*, 7-18.

> *Trusting God's providence means*
> *we stop trifling with his plans.*
>
> —CBZ

Accepting God's plan for your life depends on the quality of your spiritual life. By casting all your cares on Him (1 Peter 5:7), your anxiety will dissipate. We find that God's viewpoint defeats worry in Matthew 6:31-34, where we read:

> *"Therefore do not worry, saying, 'What shall we eat?' or 'What shall we drink?' or 'What shall we wear?' For after all these things the Gentiles seek. For your heavenly Father knows that you need all these things. But seek first the kingdom of God and His righteousness, and all these things shall be added to you. Therefore do not worry about tomorrow, for tomorrow will worry about its own things. Sufficient for the day is its own trouble."*

> *The beginning of anxiety is the end of faith,*
> *and the beginning of true faith is the end of anxiety.*
>
> —George Mueller

Hope, a Confidence That God Is in Control!

Biblical hope means confidence in the future. It's a confidence born of faith. Faith, hope, and love go together (1 Corinthians 13). When we have faith in God, we claim His promises, and they give us hope for the future. Hope for the Christian is not a feeling of "I hope it's going to happen." It's exciting expectancy because God controls the future. When Jesus Christ is your Savior and your Lord, the future is your friend. You don't have to worry.

—Warren Wiersbe.
Prayer, Praise and Promises

Relying on God's Sovereignty Results in His Peace

Believing the Lord manages everything gives us a sense of peace and freedom from the compulsion to control. *"Ah, Lord God! Behold, You have made the heavens and the earth by Your great power and outstretched arm. There is nothing too hard for You"* (Jeremiah 32:17). If we believe *"The Lord God Omnipotent reigns!"* (Revelation 19:6b), we will have comfort that He has power and authority in every detail of our lives. As the supreme sovereign and manager, no one is like God or equal to Him. Our Lord Christ's authority and power permit Him to accomplish whatever He desires, whenever He wants, anyway He wants to, and for whatever purpose He chooses according to His nature. Our God does everything perfectly according to His righteousness. Confidence in God's providence provides contentment.

The manner in which you accept God's plan for your life will determine the amount of peace in your life. If you center your life on Christ, you can have the peace *of* God. When you have the peace of God, you won't need to worry about finding someone to marry. As you wait or rely on the Lord for His will for your life, you can have His peace. You can take comfort in believing that God is working out His plan for your life.

> *When we know God's heart,*
> *we will never question His will.*
>
> —CBZ

Do You Know the Difference Between the Peace *of* and Peace *with* God?

The Bible speaks of two forms of peace—the peace *with* God and the peace *of* God. As an unsaved person you had no peace *with* God since you were at war with Him spiritually and were under His wrath; His judgment for your sin was on you (Romans 1:18). The warfare between you and God ended when you became His child through faith in Christ; then you gained peace *with* God (Romans 5:1). Peace *with* God confirms that nothing can separate us from God—no sin, no guilt, no condemnation.

The peace *of* God refers to accessing His peace after salvation. Peace in the soul is unaffected by outward circumstances or pressures. Therefore, the peace of God doesn't result from changing circumstances; instead, the peace of God is His calmness, stability, and unwavering strength amid trials. *"For He, Himself is our peace"* (Ephesians 2:14). Therefore, the peace of God comes in a person—Jesus Christ. Since God joined us with Christ, we share His peace.

Paul described the *peace of* God as incomprehensible—beyond our understanding (Philippians 4:7). Jesus told us, *"Peace I leave with you, My peace I give to you; not as the world gives do I give to you. Let not your heart be troubled, neither let it be afraid"* (John 14:27). God supplies His peace repeatedly when we trust Him because He is the giver of genuine peace that never diminishes. But what causes us to lose the peace of God?

We lose the peace of God when

- √ We are out of fellowship because of unconfessed sin. If you are unaware of sin, ask God to show you.

- √ We worry and bring tomorrow's cares into today. We may think, what will happen if..? How will I..? What if I never find someone to marry? Instead, we should think, "today's trouble is enough" (Matthew 6: 34b).

- √ We permit our focus to drift from reliance on the Lord to our problems (Matthew 6:32-33).

    When I believe that God is in control, I can relax!

How Can You Wait on the Lord?

Waiting is the most difficult when we think our need is the greatest, like during a trial or frustration of wanting to have someone to love and someone to love us. Faith rest suggests relying on the Lord, not simply waiting. He commands, *"Wait for the lord; Be strong and let your heart take courage; Yes, wait for the lord"* (Psalm 27:14 NASB). Since He alone recognizes the unknowns involved, sometimes waiting isn't waiting for His help but waiting for His perfect timing. While you wait, you can be sure that God is working out His plan for your life.

Miles J. Stanford wrote about patiently waiting on the Lord:

> I have been much struck by the thought of the concealment and slowness of God's workings. It must be a matter of distinct faith. If we do not understand this, it will make us impatient. If we understand, it will teach us to rest in God and yield ourselves all the more joyfully to Him to work out His purpose. In all creation, time is the great perfector of growth. So with us, God will perfect that which concerns us.

Waiting on the Lord means resting (stop fretting or worrying), not just waiting for God's timing. When we *doubt* that God is in control or that He can resolve problems, we strive to resolve difficulties. However, when we "let go" of the need to struggle to resolve the situation and instead roll our worry on the Lord, we are "waiting for Him." Our heavenly Father always does what is best, so expect His perfect will on your behalf. *"My soul, wait silently for God alone, For my expectation is from Him"* (Psalm 62:5). In His sovereignty, God's perfect will for you could be singleness.

> Waiting on the Lord is worthwhile because of what He is going to do for us. It is not idleness, nor is it carelessness. And it certainly isn't complacency. Instead, waiting is that divine activity of expecting God to work. And He never disappoints.
>
> —Warren Wiersbe,
> *Prayer, Praise, & Promises*

Faith Is Resting, Not Striving

Faith rest is dependent on believing the facts of the Word of God and mixing faith with His promises (Hebrews 4:2). You can have perfect peace whenever you apply this formula:

Know God's Promises + Believe God's Promises
= Enjoy God's Rest

Just thinking of a Bible verse won't help; *you must believe it.* Peace comes from believing or trusting the Lord in all matters. *"You will keep him in perfect peace, Whose mind is stayed on You,* [Why?] *Because he trusts in You"* (Isaiah 26:3). The conviction that our sovereign Lord manages everything and does what is best for us according to His plan is the assurance that boosts confidence in Him.

Faith is not a sense, not sight, nor reason,
but simply taking God at His word.
—Christmas Evans

How Does Waiting for the Lord Benefit You?

Waiting on the Lord isn't uncomplaining endurance. It isn't the same as inactivity—giving up—and doing nothing. Instead, faith resting is a mindset of living by faith—believing His promises, which are God-pleasing activities. Waiting (faith resting) is expectant faith that is quiet, restful, and confidently relies on a faithful God to do what is best. When you are trusting, you may discover that the Lord Jesus often doesn't remove the pressures until you rest quietly in Him. God may not remove the difficult circumstances, but He will always deliver you into His peace when you trust Him.

Waiting is letting go and letting God
fulfill His plan for your life.

Because God is love and He is in control, He always does what's best for us. Since God is supreme, we have no right to question what is fair or unfair. He's in control and has the power to do whatever He wills, and He's justified in whatever He does. You can trust God's sovereignty in your singleness to provide what you *need* in His perfect time.

We rest in the One on whom the universe rests.
—Miles Stanford

What Should Be Your Values While You Wait on the Lord?

While waiting listen to God's command, *"Be still before the LORD and wait patiently for him; do not fret when men succeed in their ways"* (Psalm 37:7a NIV). As you wait on God's perfect will for your life, remember God's principles.

Consider some principles from this book to keep in mind.

- ♥ Prioritize your relationship with the Lord Jesus Christ. Developing your bond with Him will benefit a future spouse.

- ♥ Keep hearing and reading God's Word, since it has the power to transform your thinking and your life.

- ♥ True satisfaction does not come from circumstances but from believing the promises of God's Word.

- ♥ Let the Lord guide and direct your life. Wait for His perfect timing.

- ♥ A complaining or discontent attitude may indicate that you don't think God knows what He is doing, that He is not in control.

- ♥ Our Father answers all prayers of the believer but only gives us good gifts—only what helps us spiritually grow. He doesn't give us everything we ask for because some things might be spiritually harmful to us.

- ♥ Friendship with the opposite sex or being married doesn't determine your significance in life. Instead, your position in Christ makes you precious in God's sight.

- ♥ View yourself as God does, as a treasure in Christ, which is where your significance lies.

- ♥ Another person will not make you complete; only Jesus Christ can do that.

- ♥ Don't rely on another to eliminate your loneliness. Jesus Christ alone can fill the natural emptiness of your soul.

- ♥ Don't presume an initial friendship will lead to something more.

- ♥ Have realistic expectations.

- ♥ Avoid obsessing with externals such as physical appearance; instead, seek a Christ-centered outlook.

- ♥ Failure to follow God's Word leaves you vulnerable to temptation.

- ♥ Neglect of His Word may lead you in rebellion against God—sin—and will bring God's discipline.

- ♥ We don't fight *for* victory; we fight *from* victory.

- ♥ Faith is the victory.

- ♥ Spend time with a prospective spouse to observe personality traits, but don't rationalize harmful flaws or overlook them. Consider whether this behavior pleases the Lord. Let objectivity guide you and avoid legalistic, rigid behaviors or opinions.

- ♥ Recognize that emotions can suggest something positive or negative. If you feel uncomfortable or anxious, this *could* be the Spirit guiding or warning you. However, emotions make fine indicators *only* when they are grounded in biblical principles; therefore, seek His truth, so you aren't deceived.

- ♥ Just because you love someone doesn't mean you should marry; God's will may suggest something else.

- ♥ Avoid infatuation—a false love, which can be deceitful.

- ♥ Marriage is a lifelong commitment—a decision to do what's best for your spouse, not just temporarily but "till death do us part."

- ♥ Some may marry without love since true love develops. Enjoyable marriages don't just happen; they develop.

- ♥ *Agape* love, God's love is not a feeling but an action that the Spirit produces through the believer who is dependent on Him; it's a mindset dependent on Him.

- ♥ In all matters of life, think from a biblical mindset of Christ first, displaying *agape* love, and serving one another.

Study Questions

Cite Scripture when possible.

1. List specific ways you are accepting God's sovereignty.

2. Where are you having problems believing in God's sovereignty?

3. What have you learned about letting God direct your life?

4. Explain how to use faith rest in your life.

Final Reflection Questions

Cite Scripture when possible.

1. How will you avoid the dangers and heartaches of modern dating?

2. God's plan may include marriage, so how will you prepare for marriage while you are single?

3. After reading this book, list the ways your perspective on singleness changed.

4. Who should be the true love of your life? How will that happen?

Glossary

***Agape* love.** Doing what is best for another in light of eternity, regardless of the personal cost to you. *Agape* is sacrificial and unconditional. This supernatural *agape* love isn't a feeling but a mental attitude that the Spirit produces when a believer is in fellowship—living by faith. This guidebook uses *agape* in the biblical sense.

Carnal. Used of the believer out of fellowship with the Lord; a carnal believer is one who follows the sin nature (self or flesh) and not the Holy Spirit. (See flesh)

Dependency. Used in the Christian life to mean reliance and subordination to Christ, which enables the believer to live the Christian life by faith, that is, the faith-rest life.

Faith/Trust. Firm persuasion, faith is the confirmation or assurance of things not seen; biblical faith is applying God's truths to your life.

Fellowship. Koinonia: communion, friendship, sharing in common, communication, partnership. Fellowship with the Lord signifies a believer following the Spirit, not the sin nature.

Flesh. Not the same thing as the body, it is "the seat of sin in man" (Romans 7:5; 2 Peter 2:18; 1 John 2:16) and is centered on self, prone to sin, and opposed to God. The flesh is the sin nature—that inborn part of human nature that seeks its own will, wants independence of God, and lives contrary to God's will (Romans 8:8-9).

Flirting. To act as if sexually attracted to someone for amusement rather than serious intent. In addition to suggestive body language, flashy, or immodest clothing, it can also involve verbal or written communication.

God's glory. The composite of His qualities that make Him holy (set apart), all that makes Him distinct and unique from all others; His radiance.

Grace. Giving you what you don't deserve, God's undeserved favor. God's grace is all that God is free to do on man's behalf because of Christ's finished cross work. In other words, God's grace is everything that God is willing to give you in blessing, apart from human merit or works because of Jesus Christ.

Heart. In Scripture, the word heart usually refers to the inner control center of a person's being. The seat of emotions is the heart (1 Samuel 2:1), the mind (Proverbs 23:7), and the will (Daniel 1:8). Therefore, we make all decisions in our heart.

Holy. Set apart as in "God is holy." God wants us to be holy—separate ourselves or set ourselves apart from sin unto God.

Infatuation. A behavior rooted in a selfish response based on strong selfish emotion; maybe a sinful response.

Mercy. Not giving you what you deserve; the loyal love of God, His faithful commitment to take care of His people.

The mind of Christ. The Word of God reveals the mind of Christ; the promises and principles of the Word of God.

The Old Man. All that you were in Adam; your position in Adam

Repent. From the Greek word *"metanoeo,"* meaning "to change your mind."

Sin Nature. See flesh above. The believer must choose between following the sin nature and yielding to the authority of the Spirit of God. Therein lies the internal spiritual battle.

Son of God. The biblical term "son" signifies that a son has the same nature as the father. In the Old Testament and other later writings, the Hebrew words used "son" to specify their relationship, not rank. God the Father, God the Son, and God the Spirit are equal in nature and deity.

The World. That organized system headed by Satan, the enemy of God. A system with godless rulers, people, teachings, ideas, and temptations that are opposed to God. Worldliness is anything that portrays sin as normal and depicts righteousness as strange.

Recommended Reading

Ashbrook, John E. *Family Fundamentals.* Here I Stand Books. 2006 Included in this book are ten ways to respect a husband and twelve ways a husband can make a wife feel loved.

The Bible, Proverbs. In this book, Solomon instructs his sons on many things, including how to choose a good wife. Women reading this book will learn what God says about being a godly wife.

Chapman, Gary. *The 5 Languages of Love* (Singles Edition). Northfield Publishing. 2017

Eggerichs, Dr. Emerson. *Love & Respect.* Thomas Nelson. 2004

Elliot, Elisabeth. *Passion & Purity.* Fleming H. Revell, a division of Baker Publishing Group. Grand Rapids, MI 1984, 2002

Harris, Joshua. *I Kissed Dating Goodbye.* Multnomah Books, Oregon, 1995

Johnson, Rick. *How to Talk So Your Husband Will Listen And Listen So Your Husband Will Talk.* Baker Publishing Group. Grand Rapids, MI, 2008

McDowell, Josh and Day, Dick. *Why Wait? What You Need to Know About the Teen Sexuality Crisis.* Here's Life Publisher, Inc. San Bernardino, CA 1987

Audio Resources

Dating, Is It Necessary? Kurt Witzig, youth pastor, Duluth Bible Church, Duluth, MN. Link at: http//www.wogbc.org/messages/?series=95

Your Identification with Christ. Presents scriptural tactics for victory over sin. Rick Gerhartz, Nov. 12, 2017. http://www.wogbc.org/messages/?sermon_id=936

Seven Considerations Before You Say I Do. by Pastor Dennis Rokser https://tinyurl.com/yb32s8o3

The Truly Christian Marriage. 39 marriage messages from Duluth Bible Church https://tinyurl.com/y9ohfhho

The Gospel of Jesus Christ
http://www.notbyworks.org/resources/multimedia/details?id=982777 (PowerPoint presentation)

http://www.wogbc.org/the-gospel/wrong-responses-to-the-gospel/

About the Author

Throughout her Christian life, Leah Weber Heling has encouraged children and adults in matters of faith. She has a passion for writing Christ-centered literature and sharing the promises of God's Word in her writing and with people she meets. Leah's practical and comprehensive writing approach to God's truths for everyday living distinguishes her from other Christian writers.

For more information about the author, Leah Weber Heling, please visit: www.linkedin.com/in/leahweberheling

Another Book by Leah Heling

LifeQuakes—God's Rescue Plan in Hard Times

Are you struggling with discouragement, depression, worry, or fear due to difficult circumstances? Discover how to have God's perfect peace, despite the troubles and heartaches of life. You will learn how to overcome worry and fear. You will discover the reasons why Christians have trials and why they are beneficial. Read LifeQuakes to understand how to have unshakeable faith when your world seems to be crumbling. *LifeQuakes* will show you how God will provide for you during a crisis, how to pray and even be thankful during a crisis, and how to draw closer to the Lord during difficult times.

If worry-free living interests you, then you'll like this Christian, inspirational guide for peaceful living by faith. Since God's Word has life-changing power, this faith guidebook incorporates the promises and truths of Scripture. Besides presenting a clear gospel, *LifeQuakes* offers an excellent explanation of the basics of the Christian life—our only hope when experiencing trials.

Reader comments include, *LifeQuakes* is "humorous as well as insightful"; "an amazing book with so much information and encouragement"; "one of the best I've ever read…helped me with my battle with cancer"; "*LifeQuakes* is well written, easy to read, understand, and apply to my life"; "I didn't want to put this book down."

Buy *LifeQuakes* to discover how to have worry-free, satisfied living, regardless of your problems. Read this book to draw closer to God and experience His comfort every day.

Available in paperback and ebook at amazon.com and other places. Amazon.com direct link: https://tinyurl.com/yauc5s3v

I Need Your Help

Thank you for reading this dating guidebook. If you found the book helpful, please take a moment to leave a positive book review on Amazon and sites like Goodreads, Barnes & Nobles, or others. Reviews help others to know about the book. Thank you.

www.ingramcontent.com/pod-product-compliance
Lightning Source LLC
Chambersburg PA
CBHW050637300426
44112CB00012B/1836